A schizphernic performance

B S BHAMRA

Published in 2022 by FeedARead.com Publishing

Copyright © The author as named on the book cover.

The author or authors assert their moral right under the Copyright, Designs and Patents Act, 1988, to be identified as the author or authors of this work.

All Rights reserved. No part of this publication may be reproduced, copied, stored in a retrieval system, or transmitted, in any form or by any means, without the prior written consent of the copyright holder, nor be otherwise circulated in any form of binding or cover other than that in which it is published and without a similar condition being imposed on the subsequent purchaser.

A CIP catalogue record for this title is available from the British Library.

ART

A schizophrenic performance

Part 2

B S BHAMRA

Published in 2019 by FeedARead.com Publishing

Copyright © The author as named on the book cover.

The author or authors assert their moral right under the Copyright, Designs and Patents Act, 1988, to be identified as the author or authors of this work.

All Rights reserved. No part of this publication may be reproduced, copied, stored in a retrieval system, or transmitted, in any form or by any means, without the prior written consent of the copyright holder, nor be otherwise circulated in any form of binding or cover other than that in which it is published and without a similar condition being imposed on the subsequent purchaser.

A CIP catalogue record for this title is available from the British Library.

Hello my name is benjmasin benson singh bhamrai am the writer author and artist 0of trhis bo0ok I am curently sufferimng from a well known phycratric illness called schizopherina as you already and probably know there a a few types that we could be suffering from as it goses for mine I have the worst paaranonoia I am a parniosd schiozophernic. Ok do not worry I can tell by the look on your face you are not to impressed well do not worry i9t is common that we can over come the desease in mind has no cure however it can be cured with t7he ringht manage ment so do not friet you cannot actch the aaaaathe dease it is someething you are born with.

The book below with siome of my pictures are there to sooth you and heal you if you look at them in the right way I as an writer and author of this book leave myslef open to oppinion and critisiusm. Not everything in the book trhat I have painted well it might not mesan that much to you and other pitcures might. I am thinking that I wmat this book to be you.

ART

A schizophrenic performance

Part 2

B S BHAMRA

Published in 2019 by FeedARead.com Publishing

Copyright © The author as named on the book cover.

The author or authors assert their moral right under the Copyright, Designs and Patents Act, 1988, to be identified as the author or authors of this work.

All Rights reserved. No part of this publication may be reproduced, copied, stored in a retrieval system, or transmitted, in any form or by any means, without the prior written consent of the copyright holder, nor be otherwise circulated in any form of binding or cover other than that in which it is published and without a similar condition being imposed on the subsequent purchaser.

A CIP catalogue record for this title is available from the British Library.

Hello my name is benjmasin benson singh bhamrai am the writer author and artist 0of trhis bo0ok I am curently sufferimng from a well known phycratric illness called schizopherina as you already and probably know there a a few types that we could be suffering from as it goses for mine I have the worst paaranonoia I am a parniosd schiozophernic. Ok do not worry I can tell by the look on your face you are not to impressed well do not worry i9t is common that we can over come the desease in mind has no cure however it can be cured with t7he ringht manage ment so do not friet you cannot actch the aaaaathe dease it is someething you are born with.

The book below with siome of my pictures are there to sooth you and heal you if you look at them in the right way I as an writer and author of this book leave myslef open to oppinion and critisiusm. Not everything in the book trhat I have painted well it might not mesan that much to you and other pitcures might. I am thinking that I wmat this book to be you.

I would go back after taking a second look at it and then I would say I do not loike it and then I would look at it gain and then I would say I klike it. Over gain and again simple answer for all of that comotion over this particular picture is the fact that I could not make up my mind if I did or did not loike what I have painted. What do you think

As for this part of the book and the art in question is the offer of what is below worhthy of being in my book I have to admit the the iead below did not really catch my eye tyet it is still there anoyher picture gone terriblely wrong in my eyes I am almost embarecsts by the picture as much as I mght trhink although that's just my own personal veiw you as the viewer might bring it back to life if you cou;d see some thi9ng that I have not. orginal painting £ 150 print £ 75 the idea was to make the picture above look like a comic book cover I personally think tht its great as I would being my work alytjpougvh i9 do have a large comic book collection so I would I do not thinks its is that bad as for a firsttime efrfort and it's the only o0ne that I have attempted to paint so its an orgianl in that sense. In fact I have told a lie I do have another comic book cover you wi;ll find it below.

Orginal painting £ 150 print £ 75 my buetiful pitchure of wht looks like to me are the plat plains of what is left of the ice pole at nightime or if you could imagine being driven past an extre,ely flat place. At nightime. The wwiew ouyside of the window looking out form within. £75 whay you see here are two abstract pitures the first would be an abstract pitchure the second would be an abstract picture of two seats in a bus at the back of the bus to the left a window and there is no right strach your imanagination, can you see what I intended you to see. £75   here is a good piece of mine at the mpomengt it is still unfinished and I have to say in my mind it looks good there is around several different ways I will approach this piece this is just one so if you see it again and agin you will klnow why and this was on my first atempt. No colour just design and figureing which way I ws going to put the pieces of art together if I cpuld put the rest of it right ill show you in the next book some thomng to think aabout and wait for it has no name at the moment just like the others infact I have not named any of the pictures in this book for sucurity reasons hust that word makes it feel speacial. Design sketch £150 i the general idea here ws to cfreates a piece called the pino what you have in front of you ids the painting but it is in three parts the orginsal version is framed and in hiding in my bedroom tht gives the game away a bit but still its long like the pino hence the name also it has a second part of the nsme to it again because of the lengh this piece would set you back about five thousand pounds however that's the price that I dreamt of putting it at however ill let it go for a hundread and twenty.

two faces theb man in the shop how the paintiung bacme him I do not know £75 print   the pictures below and above are parts of my mind as I am trying to paint not knowing what I was trying to create and kind of lost my way this happens to me some of the time I will paint or design and it all goes wrong. What we have at the bottom and the top are two really good examples of what my worst efforts was. Even though the bright coilours pulling me in to it and frowning as I am looking like I have lost my way my only thought is to destroy them I am in two frames of mind as all I can say that it has to exsist as it came frommy mind and gods.

these two pieces are two better examples of my work the top one first looking at it in four different ways it is bringing life to wards my vision oiam not sure what I was trying to create it s all the brushes works and it did work in trhe nd it is like a vivid sunset or like clouds movin a land scape or some thing alongs those lines I cannot really tell you much more I think that I will call it yellow clouds £125 print £25 depending on size The piece below abstract two lines and a small square it was as simple as that £125 print £25 depending on size. i I have created this thi9ng above I have no idea of what is it meaning I am leaving it to your imagineation however now that I have taken a resonably good look at it it nows grows on me and im thinking that its not that bad now. £ 150 -print - £ 75. Depending on size.

this piece is one of my favorites when it is not on it s side my abbsrtct face it's a orginal b bhamra it almost looks like a slupture I can imagiune it in clay or plaster of paris its worth some trh9ijng to me as the artist that created it not availibkle in clour however that wowuld kaje a difrerence as I wanted it just as I created it and it does the whole idea of everything that I have discussed above it almost looks lonley and it stands like it is on one leg and the emptyness of the piece as it stands a lone. This piece will cost you about £ 165 nand a print £ 75 depending on trhe size. this is an akward one I had just had my hair done and and I was th8inking of the coul;ours that I have chosson herre it says ragga to me jamica and it works if you can look at it for a long period of trime inspired by rasta clours of the jamacan flag I have not turned this one up side down yet so I only have one perspective of this particualr piece £ 150 and £75 print depending on what size. this is interesting my first or one of them to try and create a axctual this is the view form my sstudy cross living room window drwn about 2020 nad I have a few of these infact this is what I am focused on at the moment and I trying to perefect it. Oringal print £150   d put them together to make it look like a atreet in order to

ctreate a picture so it looks like a street with lots of houses this is the orginal copy of the print £299 original print. I have yet to price up the full
picture once created I have used one picture and created it again
An

This concept of my art the message that I wanted to
semd out throw my work and it was woerking until I
ran out of luck one moment I was being asked and
evrybody was happy then I was cut off finding mysllef
at a lost nobody wanted to veiw or look at my work old
froieds in the back ground and officals at the stern
giving me little hope of the second experdition which I
was clingning to as for the publicity and it would be the
importtant peole the countcilors and then other artosts
but yet a again I ahad fbailed only to be able to sell a

print and not a pianti9ng two to a friend I still dream as I wait to meet her gagain to find out weather dshe really enjoyed it as much as I enjoyed her mmoney as I did. Then the place where it all started in hospital I was crying out like I have explaianed all year for some space yet I wa soffred and then declined denied declined I ws upset ait was haard enoufh with the whole world on your shoulders but to be sent awayaftyer being promised and approached was a little bit dishearteneding however I still had the balls to follow it up only to be sent around inj circles and get no where the idea of wanting to ecxhibit within the council was now a turn off I still think it is them getting there own back ignoring my tallent for not wanting to speak for them ay there seminar. It's a dirgty game and ill be honest id enjoy their dirtyness as I would enjoy my own business it sucks peoe around me say im good at it I have declined everything and every deal that has ever been made to me and ill agree that is not a a lot however I still say that I am a great artist and business man.

Going back to the fun, aart my largest piece to date 2020it lights up my mind with a gigantic powerful use of colour splatered eceverywhere and anywhere I could fit it on to the large painting which started off as a painting and became a super gigantic print. Im in control I dont like it I love it I want it and wear is it going as it too now is taking me on a n adventure.

In trhe beginning it was just a bit of fun as I look back at the art that I created as a teenager it was so appualingly bad I had no time for it ill introduce to you the painting mostlly in acrylic paint and pastel their was onecea time not so far agao that I would be in a class room not to shy of being imbarest that I would draw and colour an africa abstract village and then giant grass hopper and then as I rember a tradage piece ill call it the openiong of pandorias box ill leave it as tat for now.

As it goes for all of my art as I grew the art and what I saw grew differently I was for a long time traped in the idea of drawing eyes. Eyes in the sky and on the oceans and many time s I told myslef that it ws wrong therer was something about the pictures it they were almost child like it was not too long befokre a found my fellow artist distroying them in front og=f my very eyes. As for what was left I would like to say it left me in and with alots of room to improve.

Now I have seen ennough through my mind to cretae my next hundred pictures some of them ggo I like them others I just thought it was a waist of time and even thougvh peole would comment on them I sure it ws hard to beleve in my eyes that every comment and compliment was given ws one of emfusiasm and that they were good I idid not believe the commnets that's werer made my art another in dephed solutions to ithe idea that I shpould starave myseeeelve just so I could get a better pitiure it would imspisre me not just as anartist but as a writer. Im good your good they are all good but one thing I now know is that they do not care and in the short future my art work will if I can produce show you why. I think I am talking about what I know no.

And hit the floor hard as I find myseelf painting the same things and in my mind told me to try something else as I did I found that I could use more colours I would usely stick on only to four my be five at this stage.

Ok so as I travel through my mind only to see that the moving images that control me are none chnmagijng and for me now a little boring and upseting and frightening as I create and try new ideas I seemed to have fallen down.

Olk so find myslef createing werid things odd shpes and werid faces tyhinbs that at that time ment nothing but looking at them hard and in different ways made and makes them work this is me this is my art worrrrrk the lights are on the camera is fixed and the paint and brushes are fuueld another new concept is going to be the eyes balls it had occurred to me a while ago however it did not go to0 far as I only magaed to complelete one drawing and it lies doormant with the rest of the unwmated on good badly dre=awn. However I thinking about bring that one picture out its good its smart and its will hity the abstract world with a bang just the in the same way t6hat gid made the earth. I hope that was not too sacrillighious I have a bettr image which will be in the making veery soon.

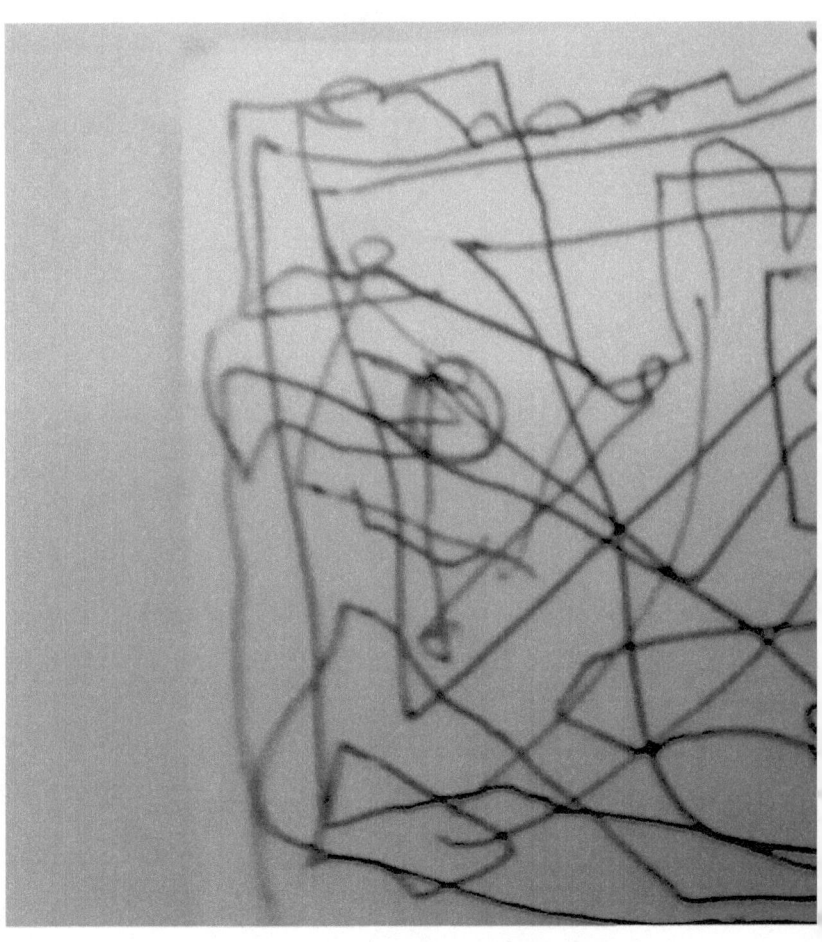

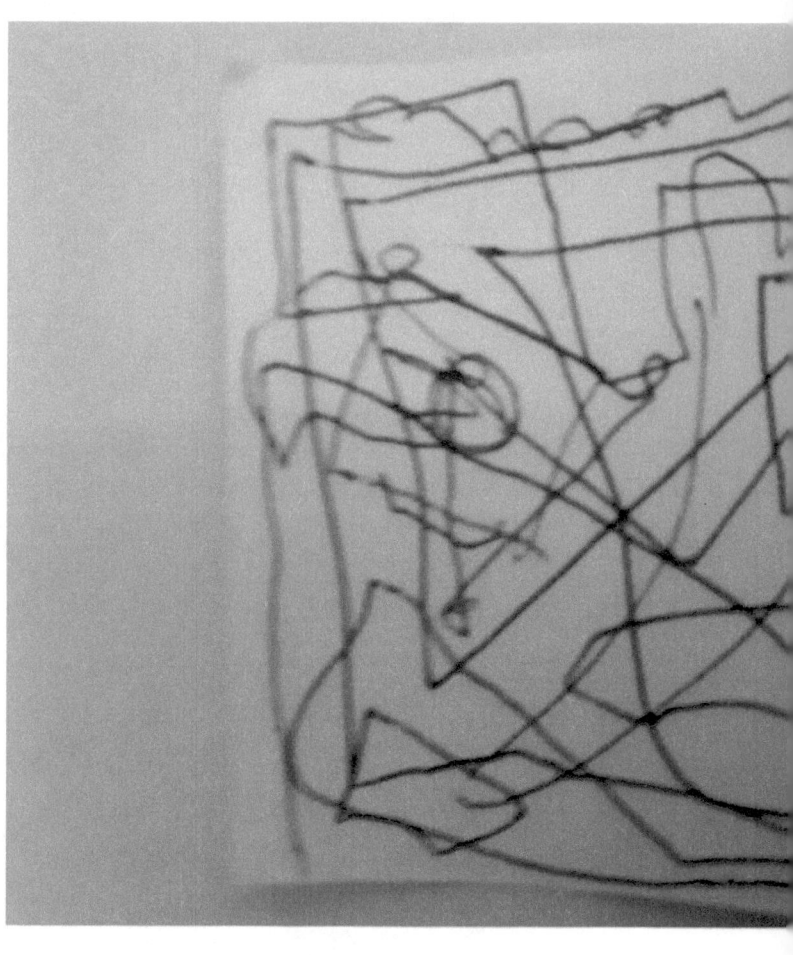

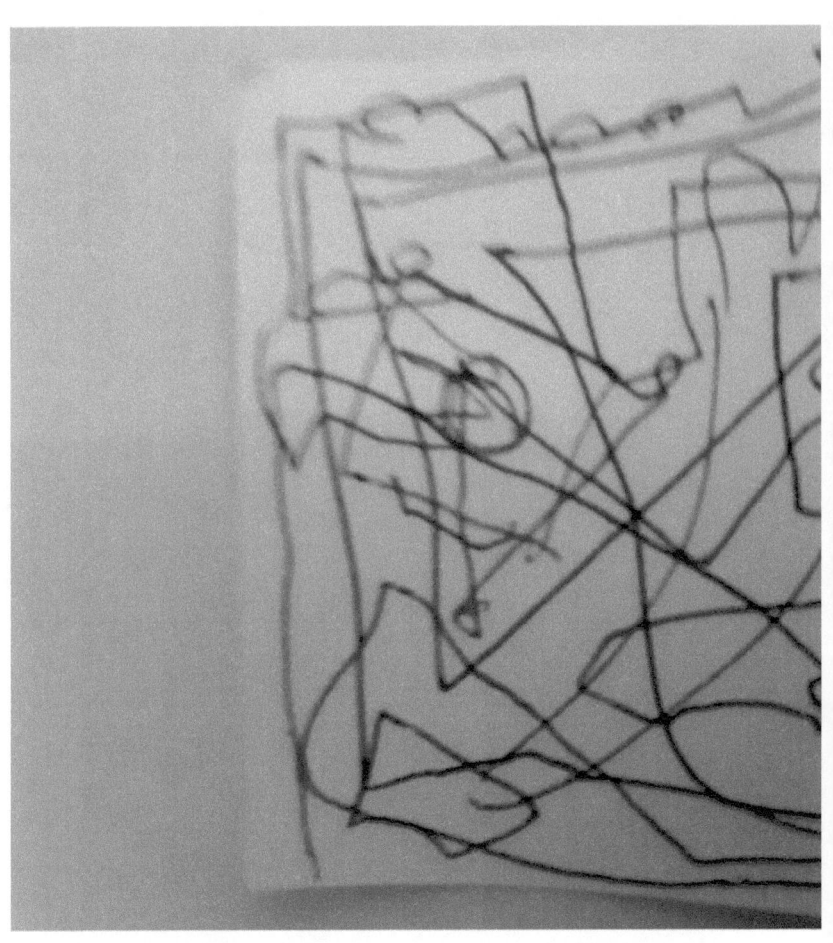

his particualr

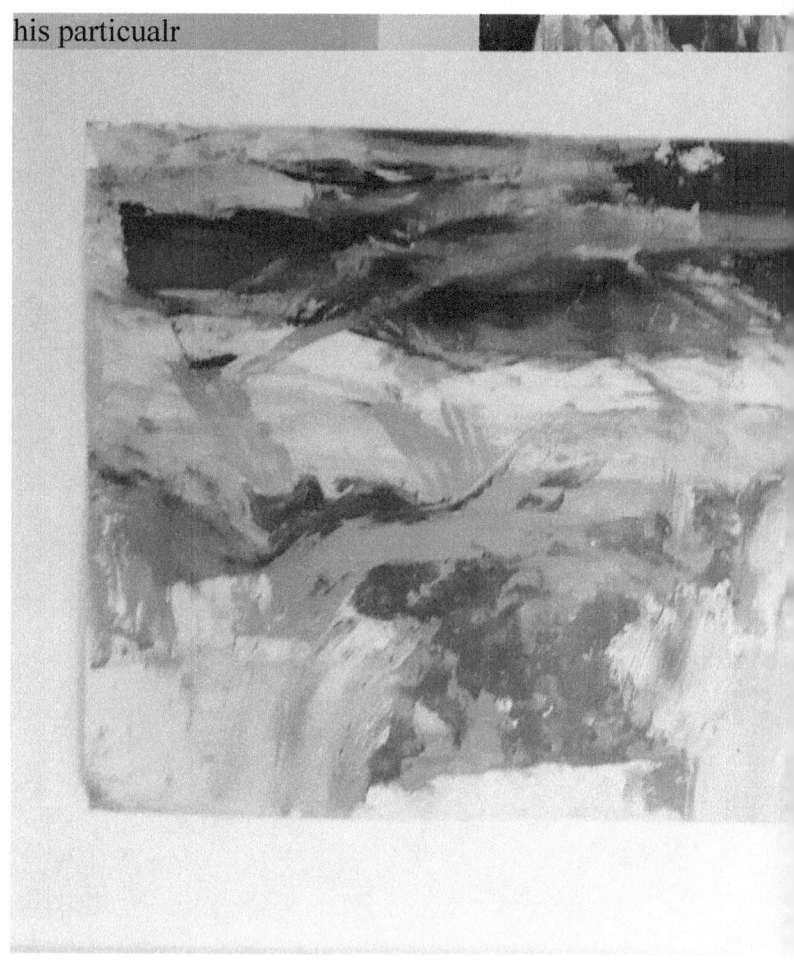

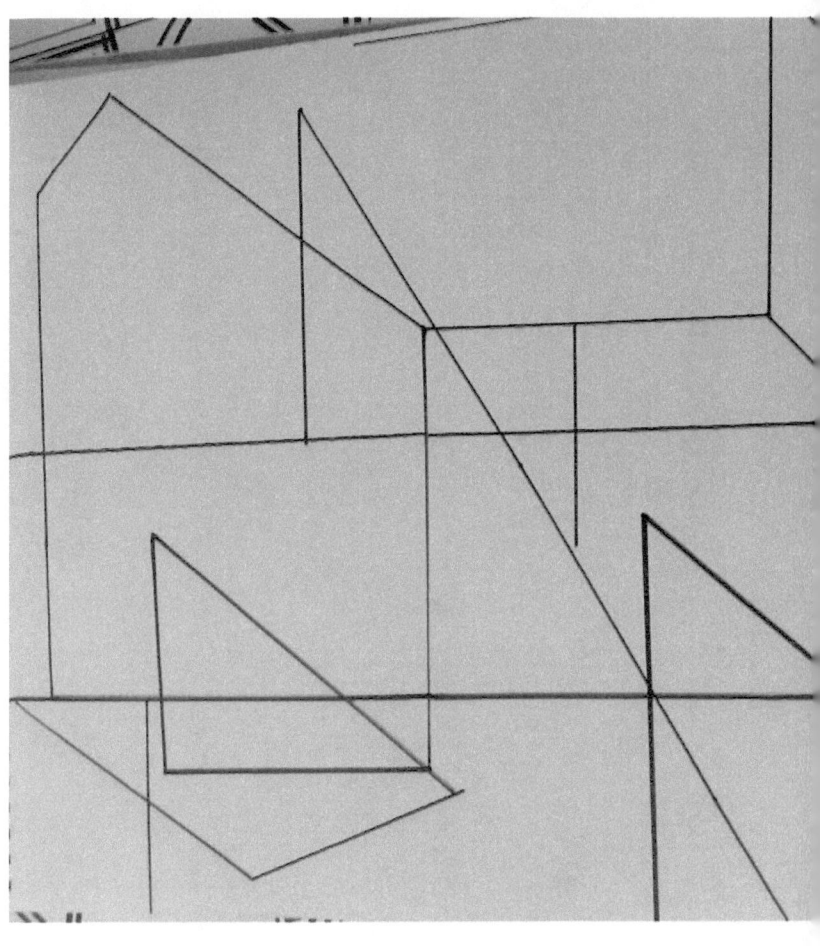

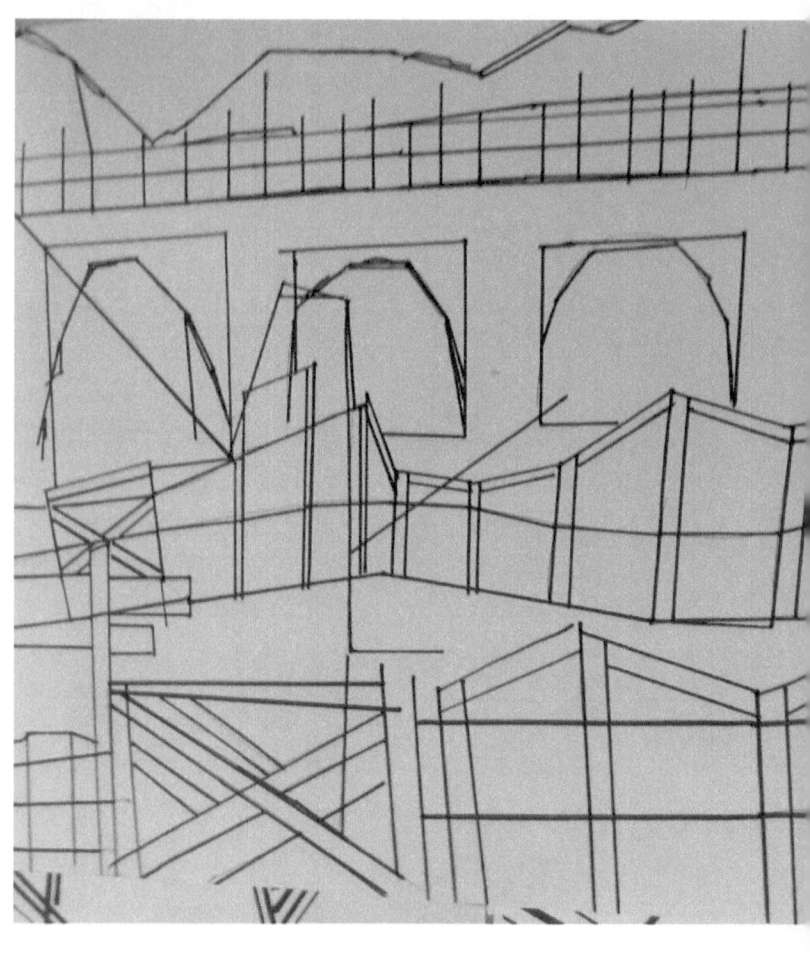

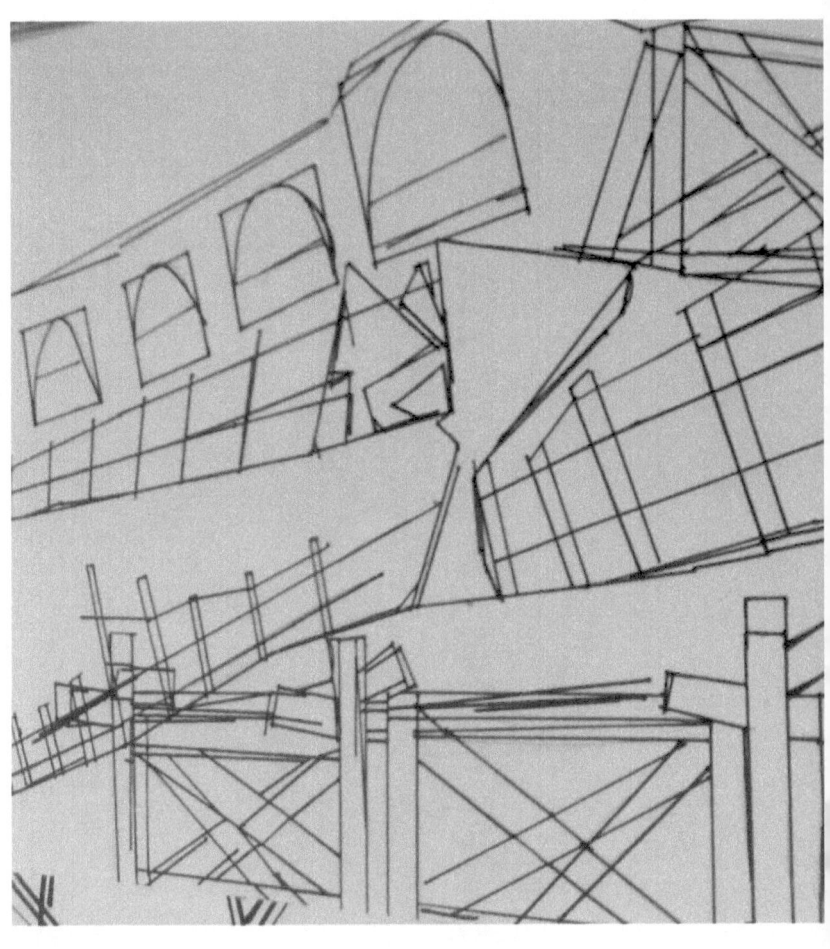

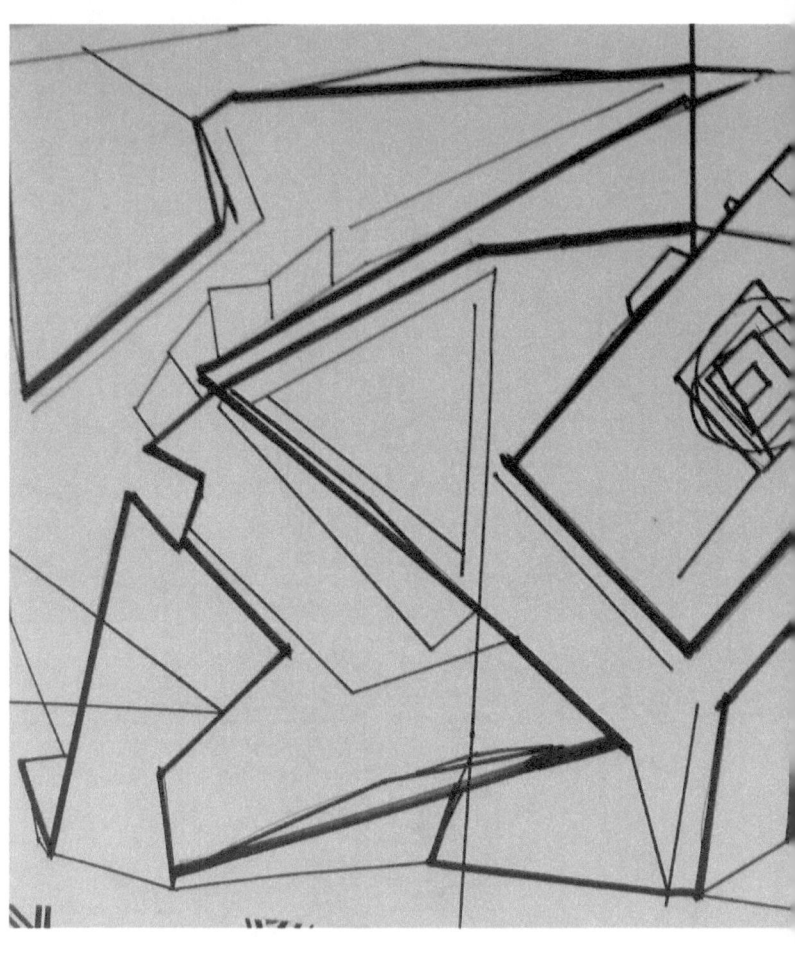

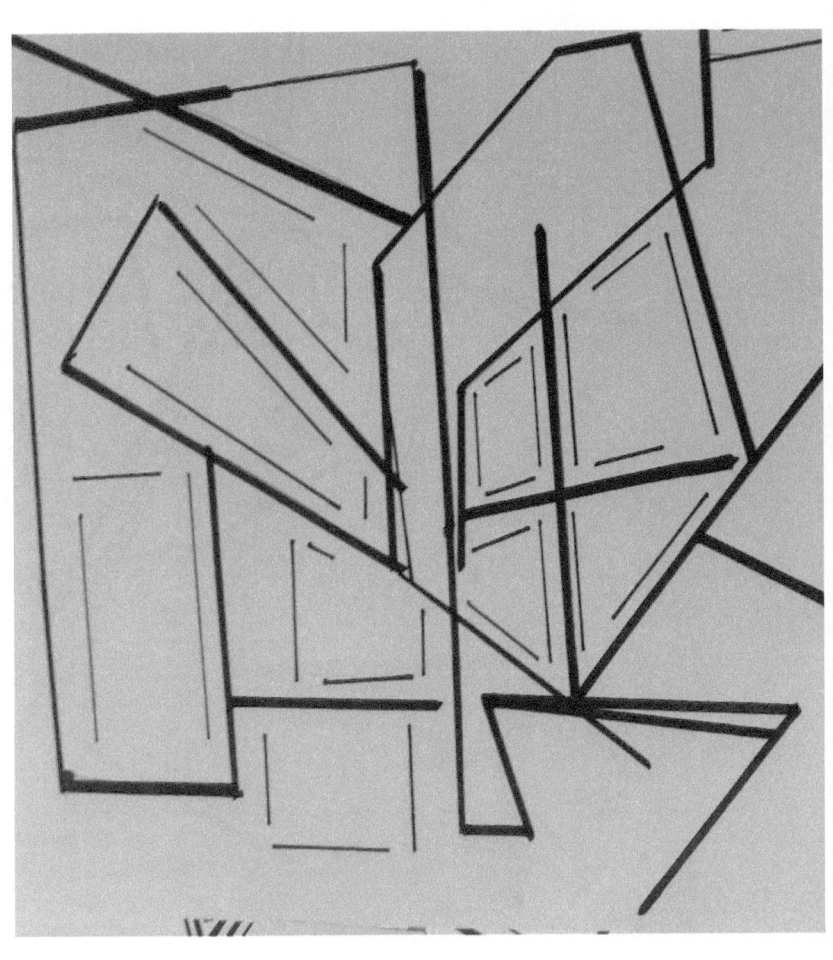

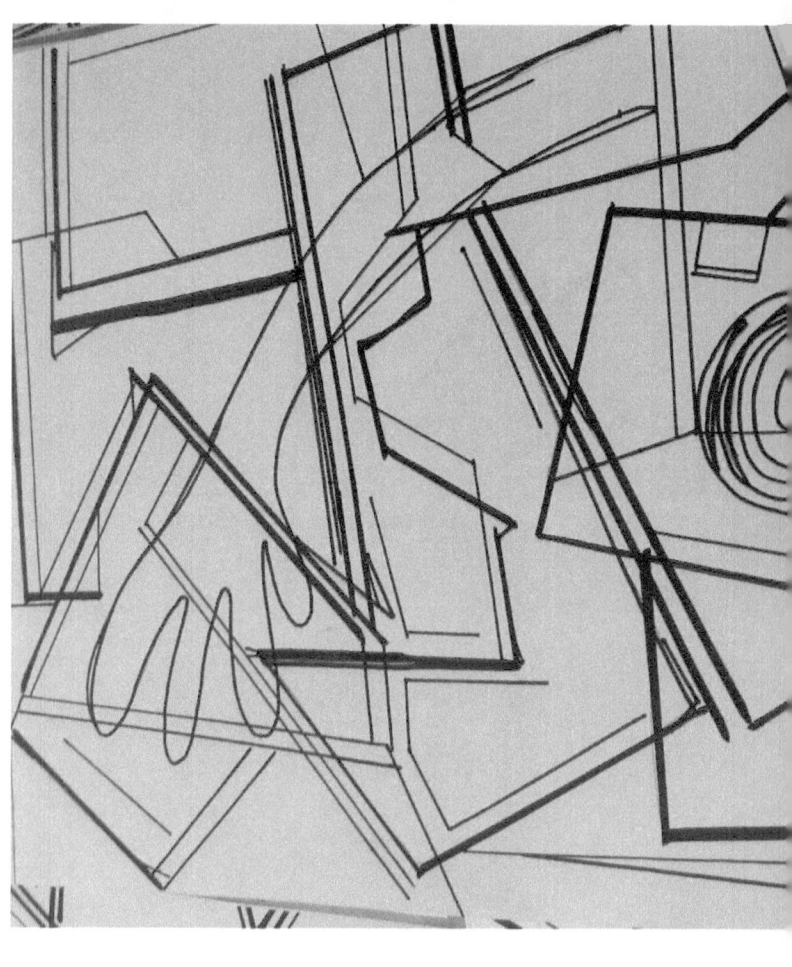

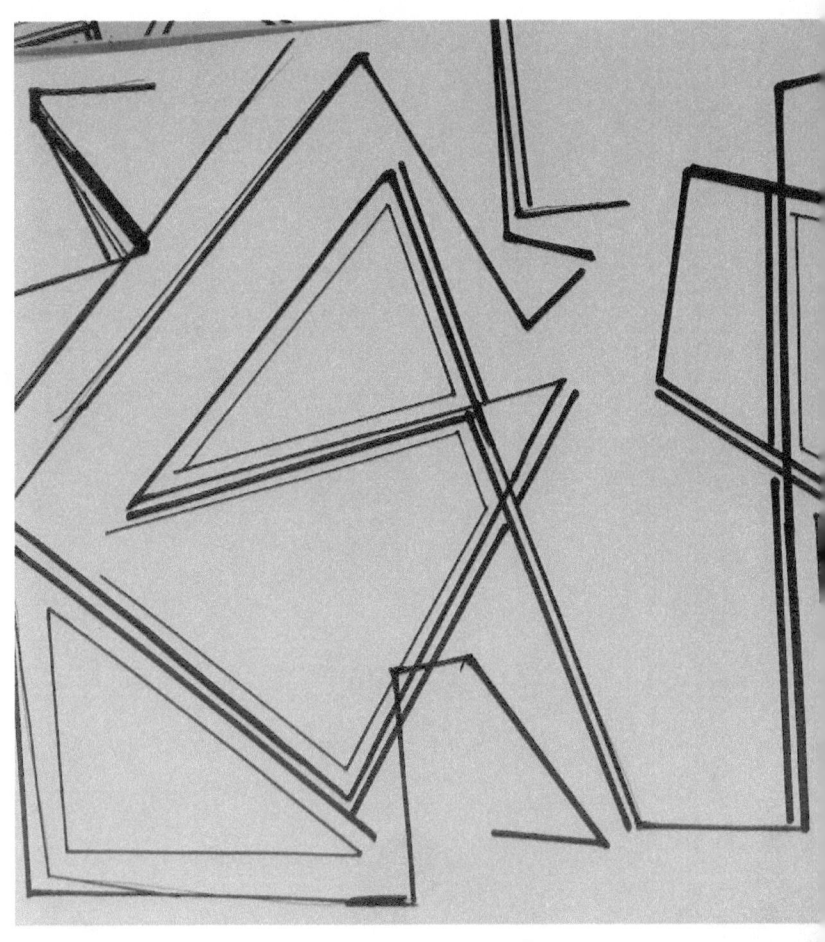

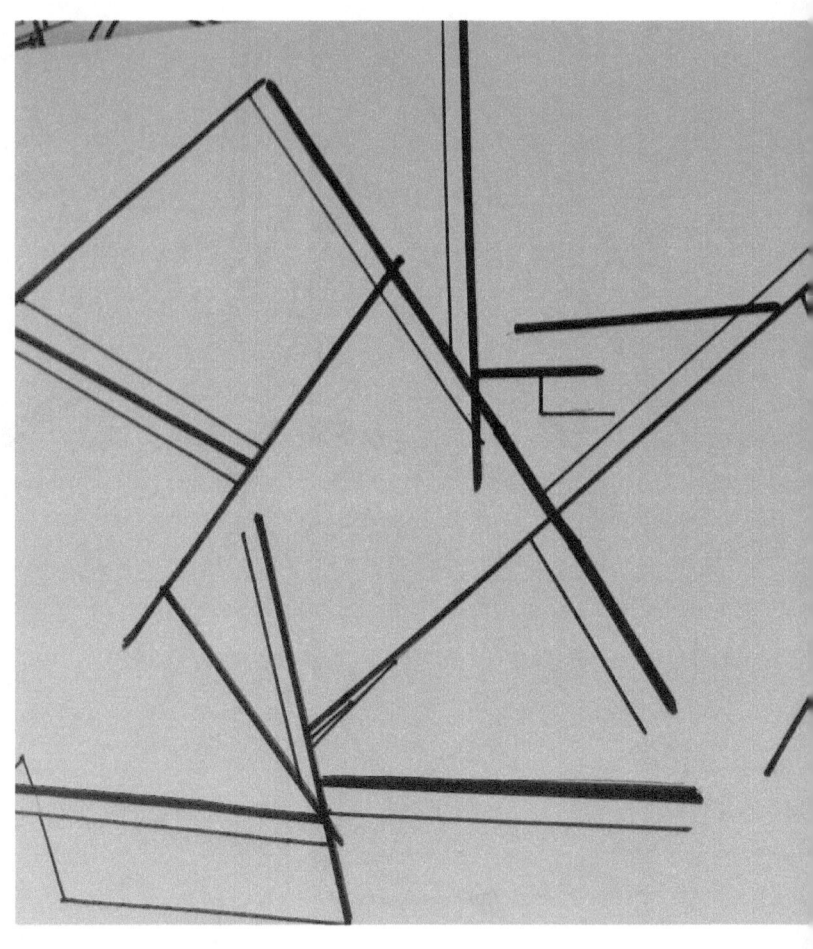

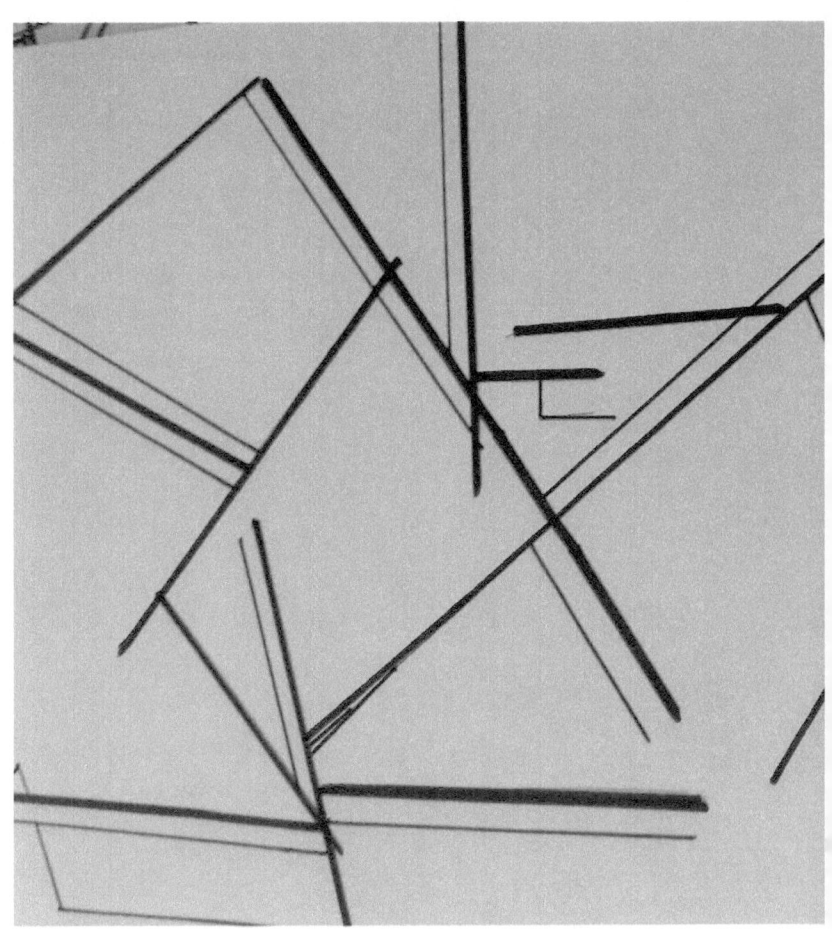

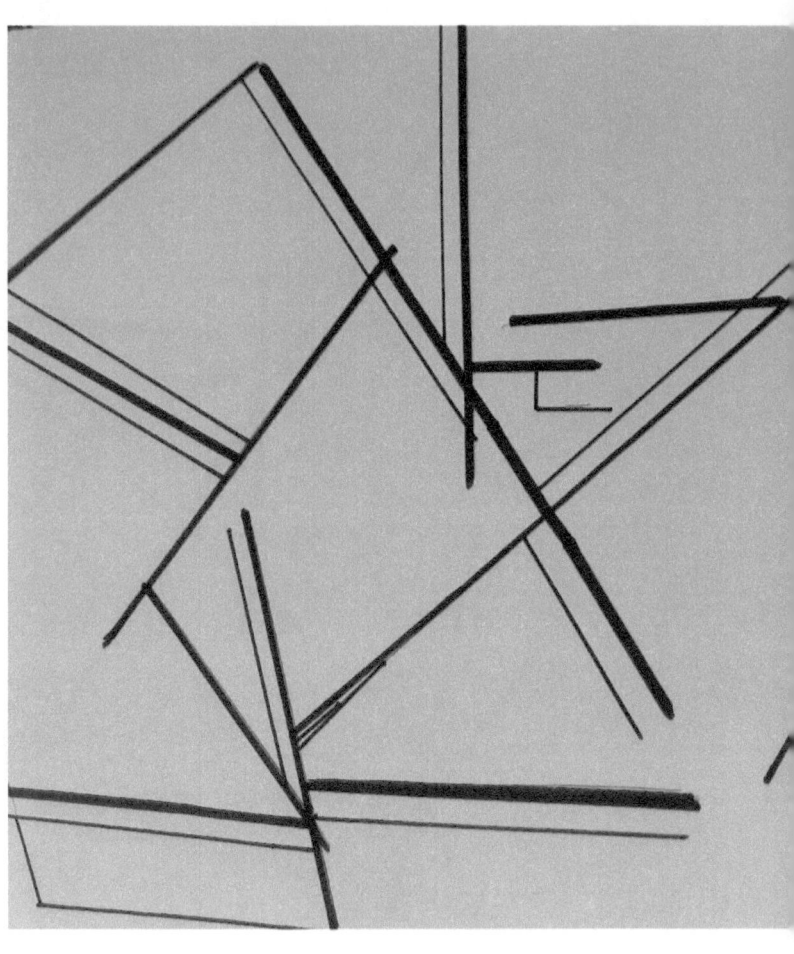

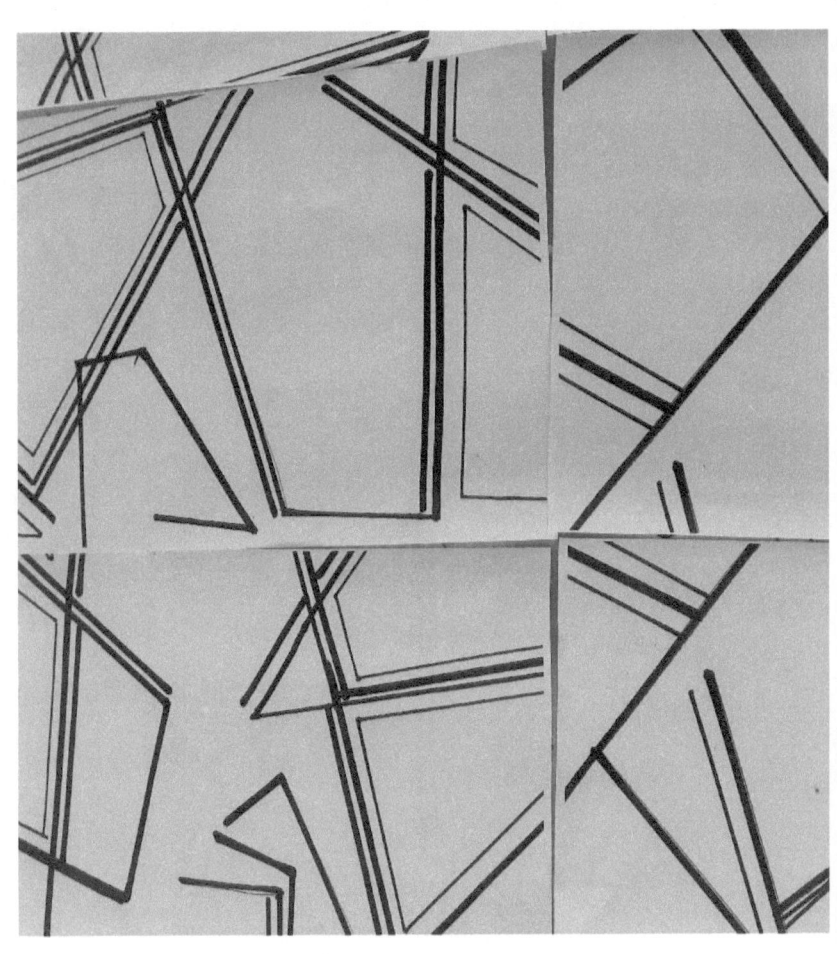

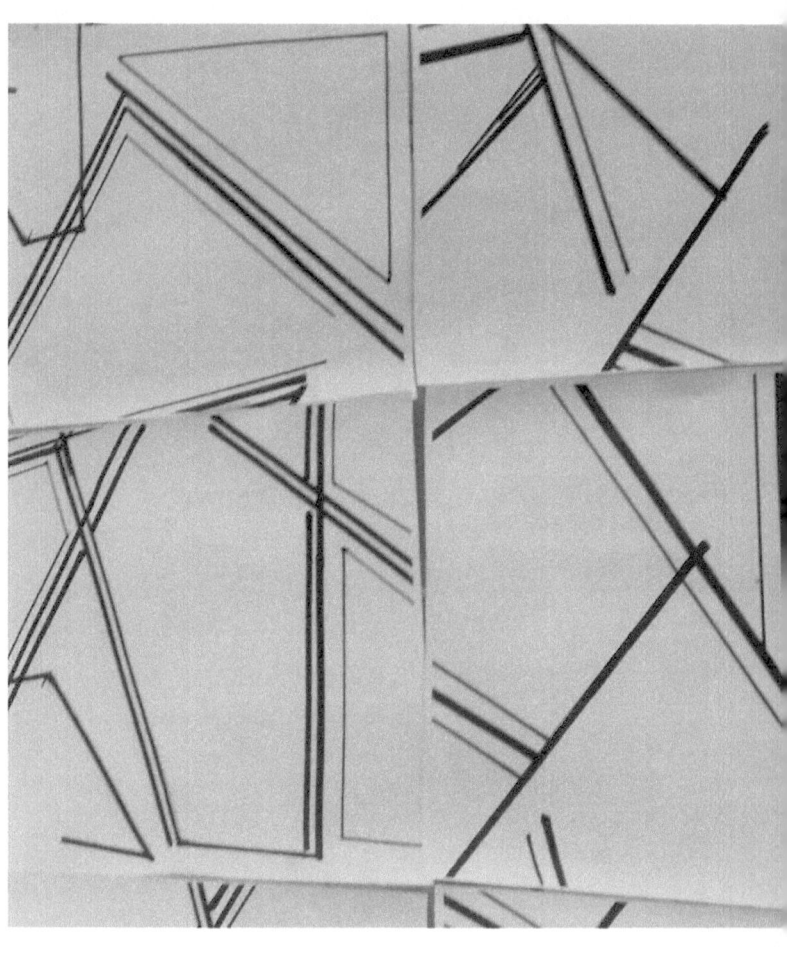

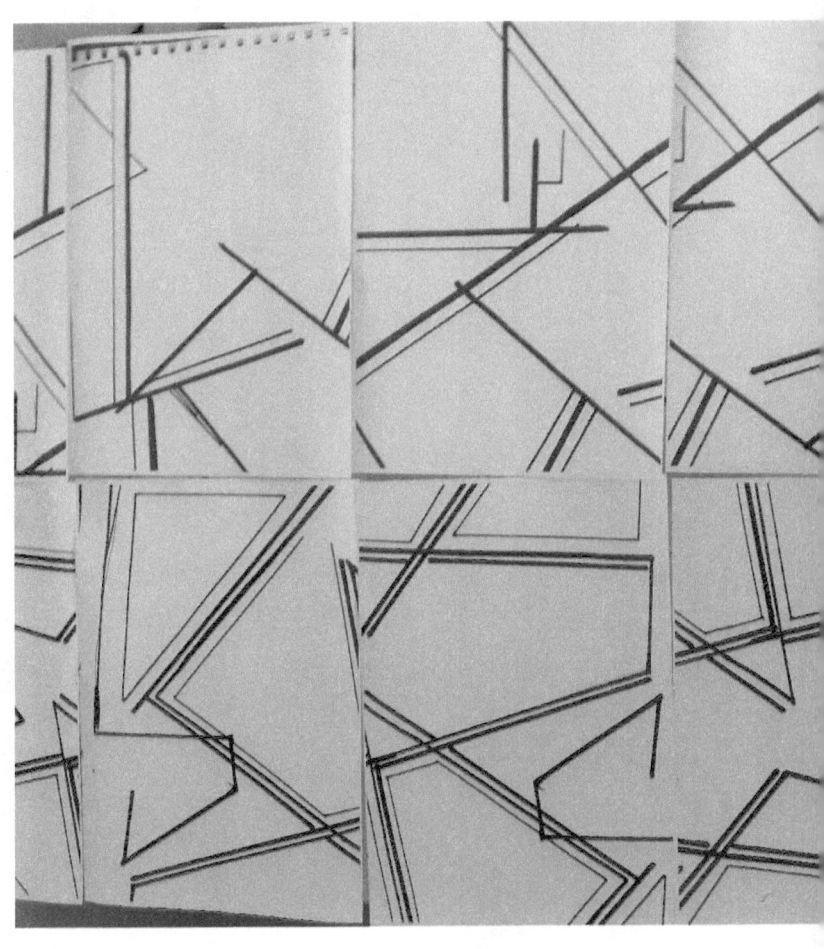

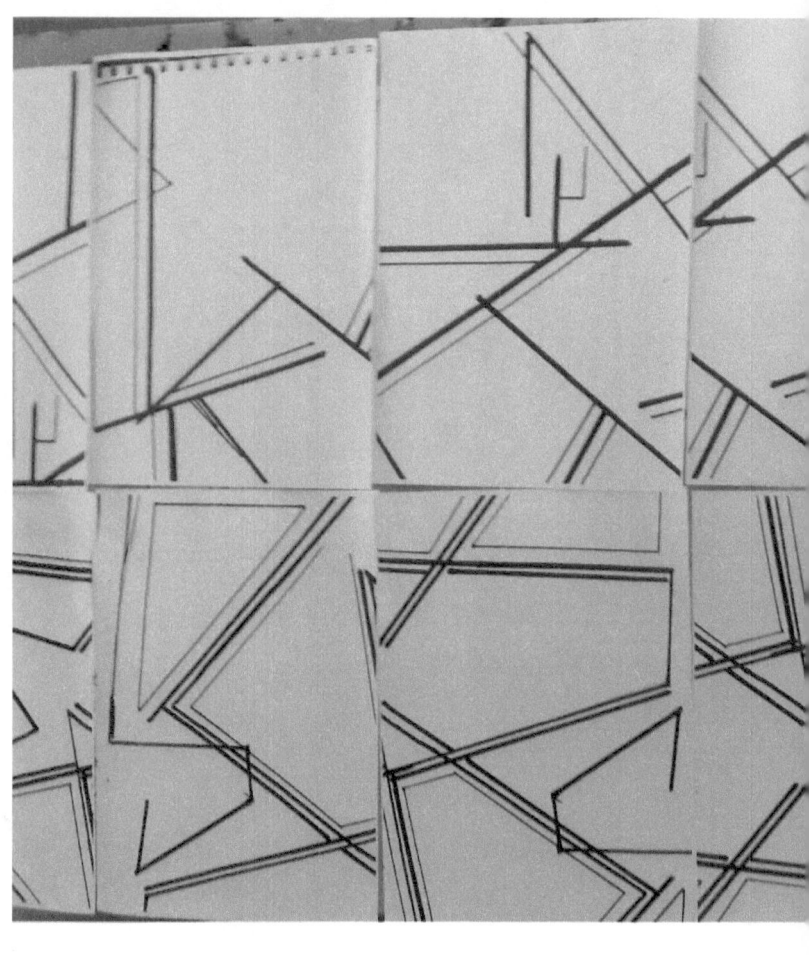

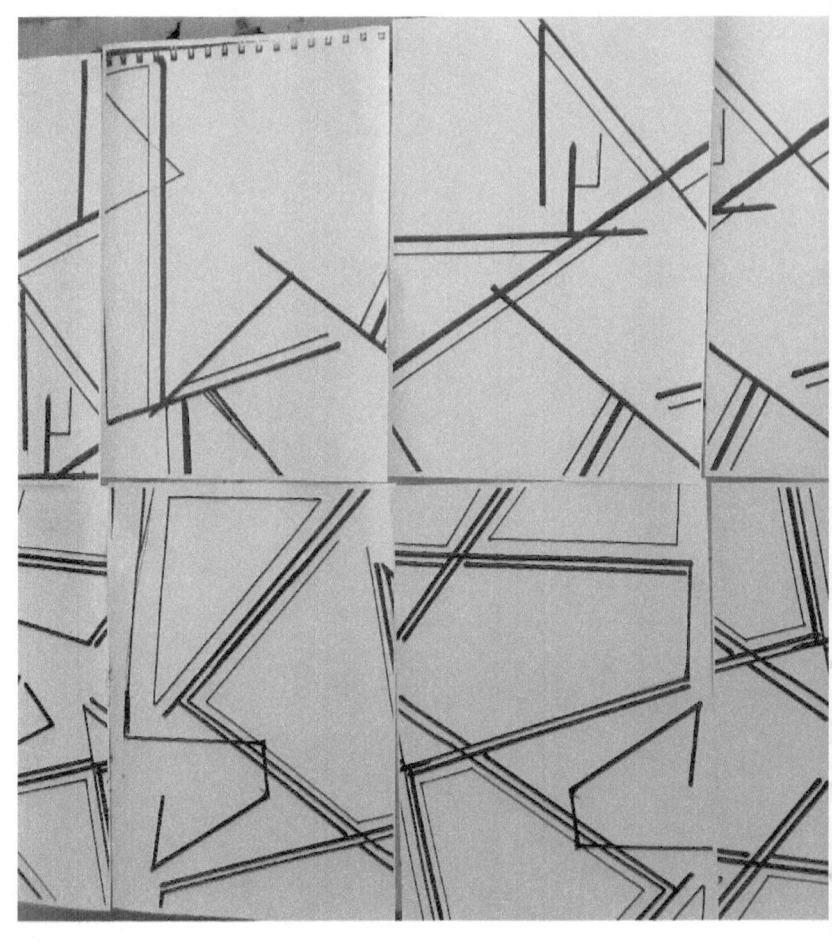

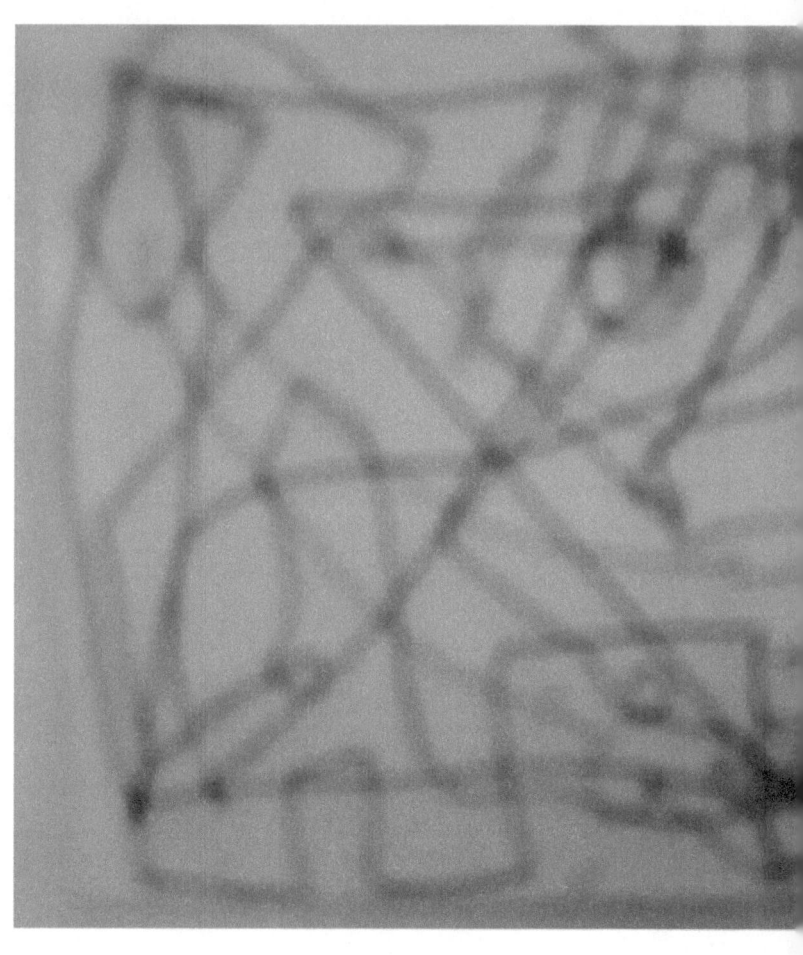

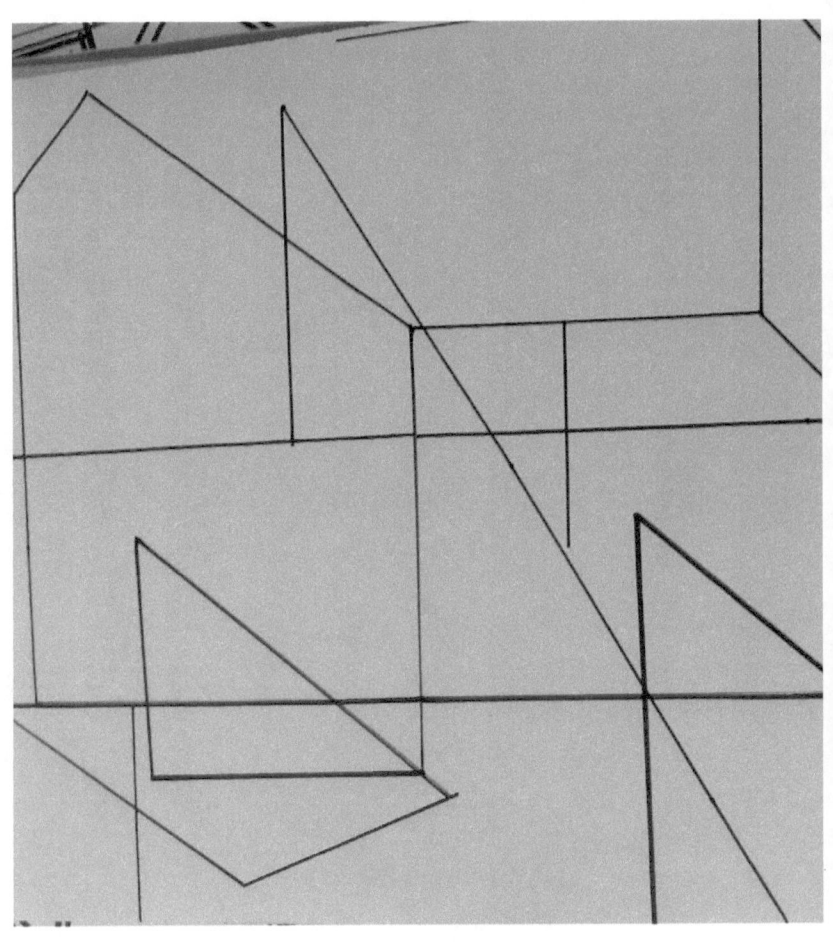

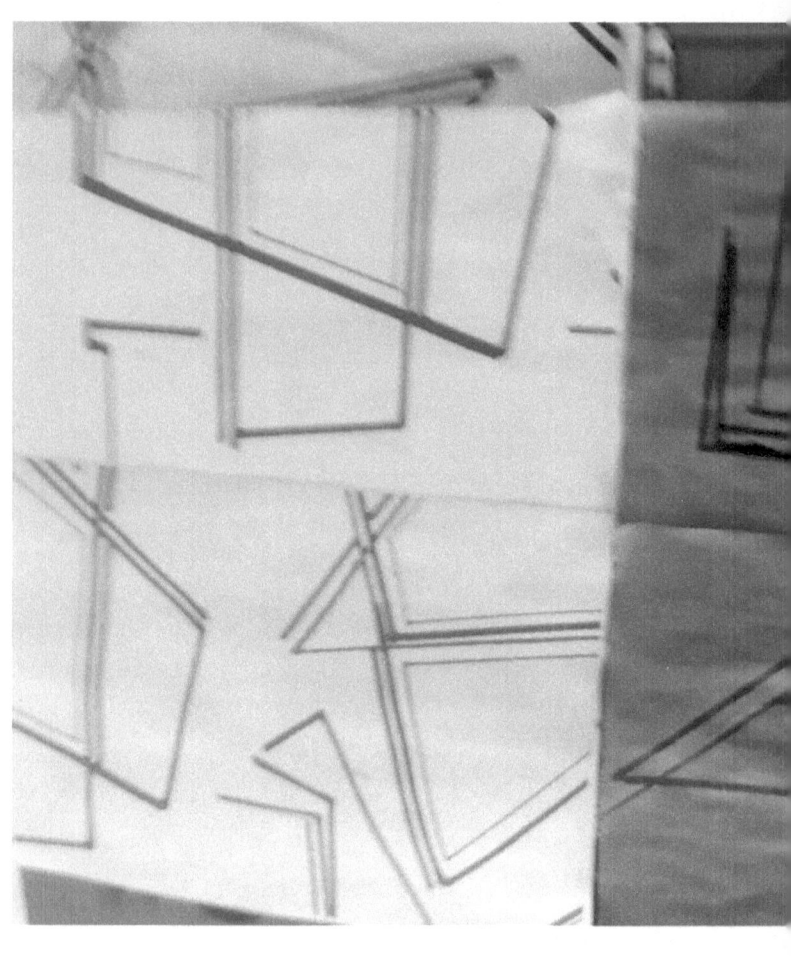

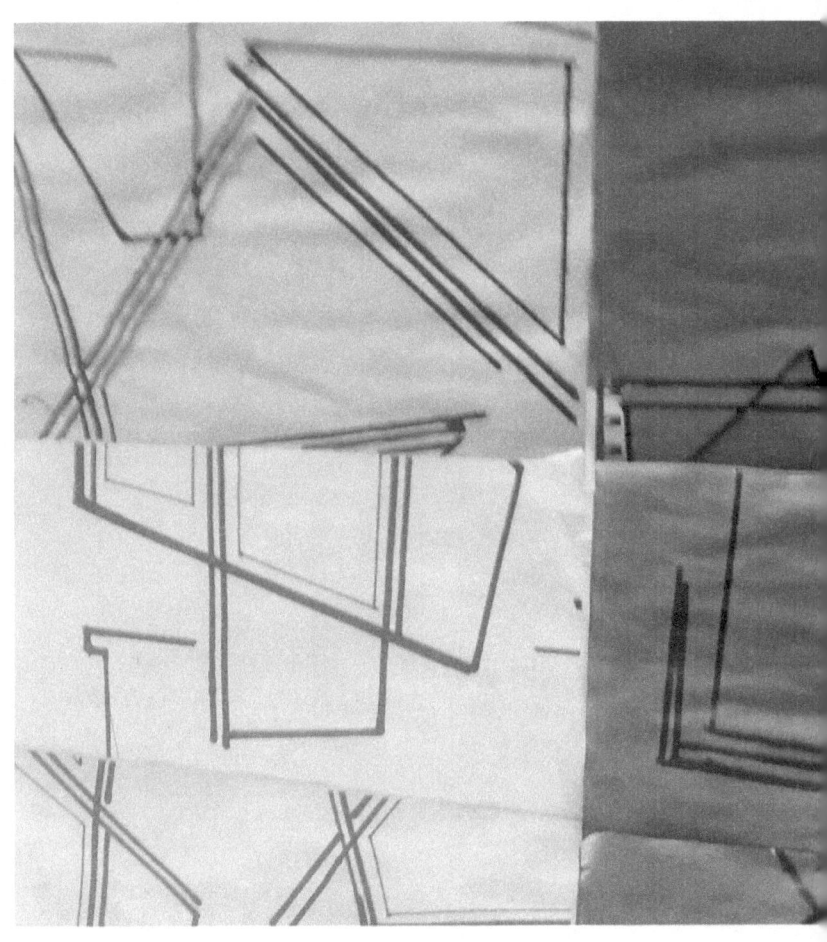

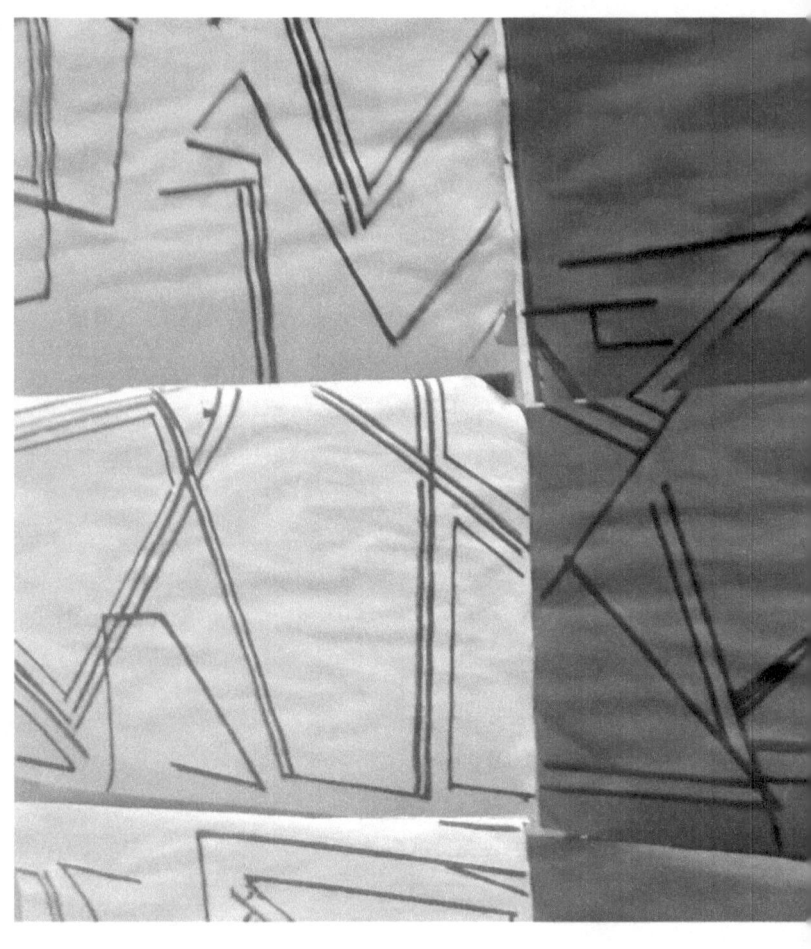

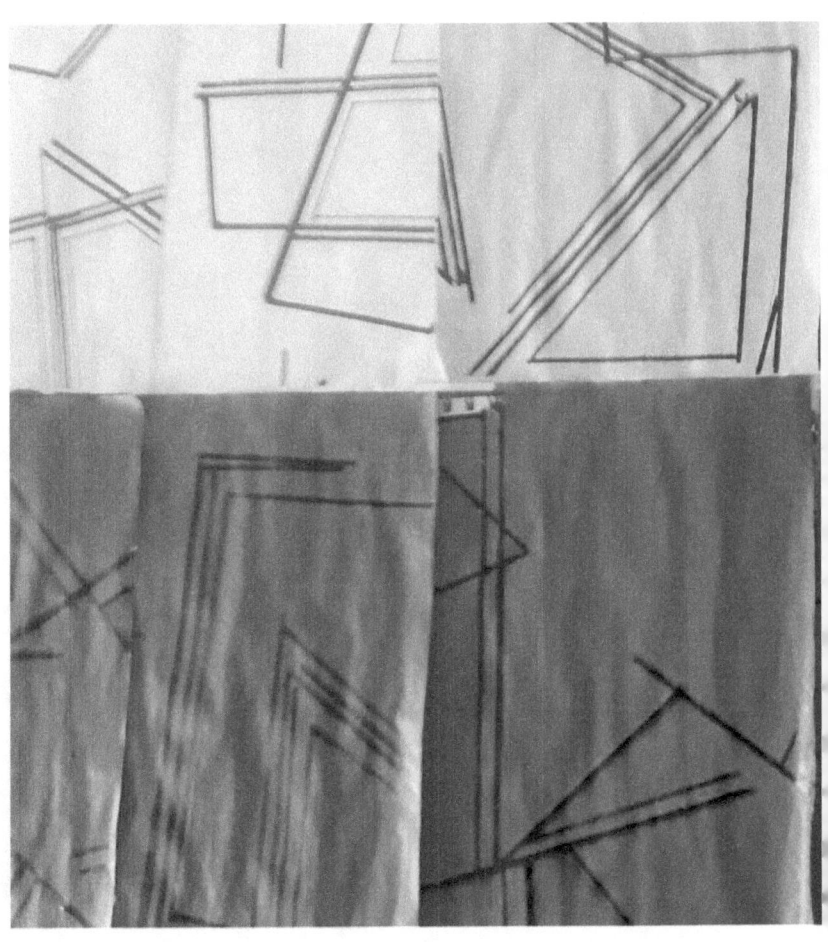

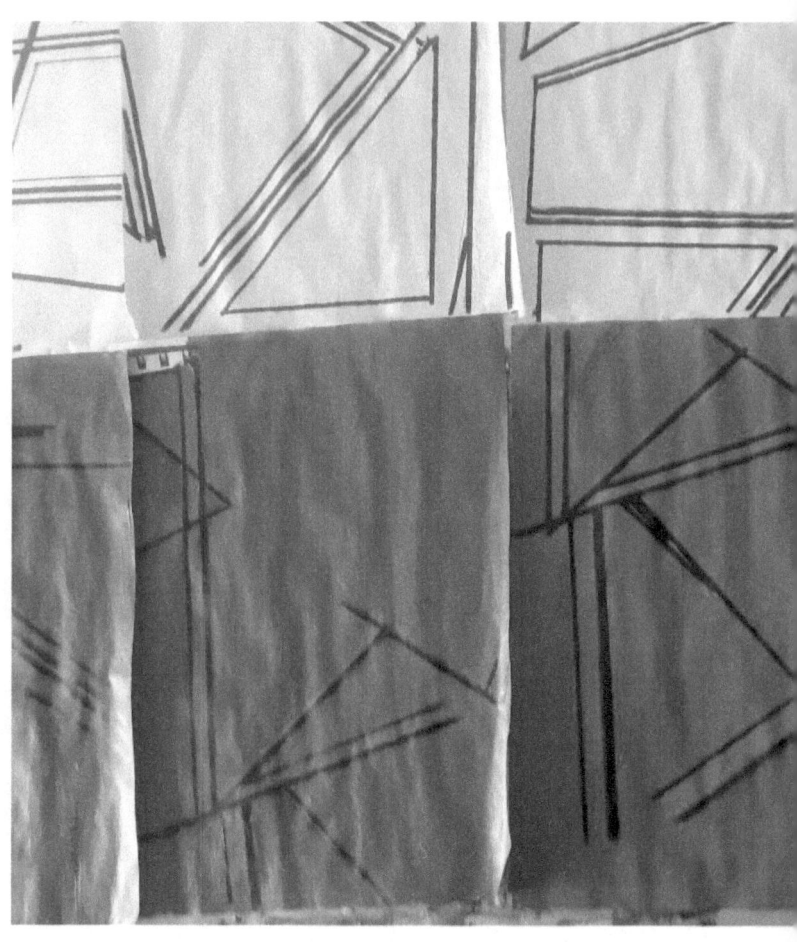

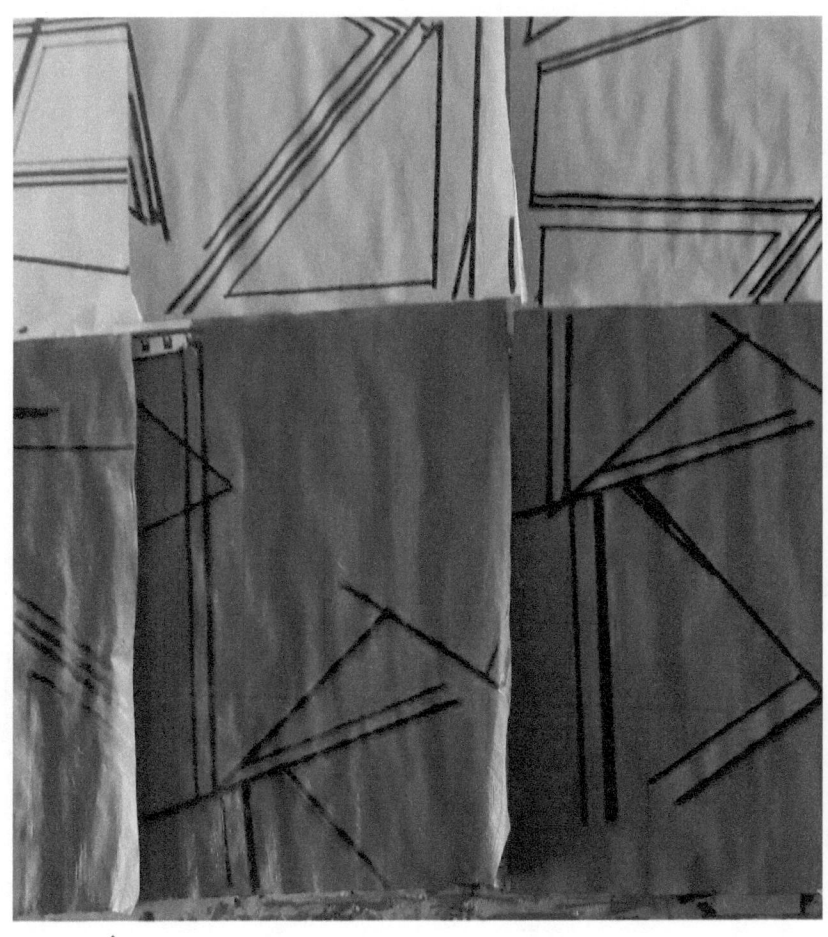

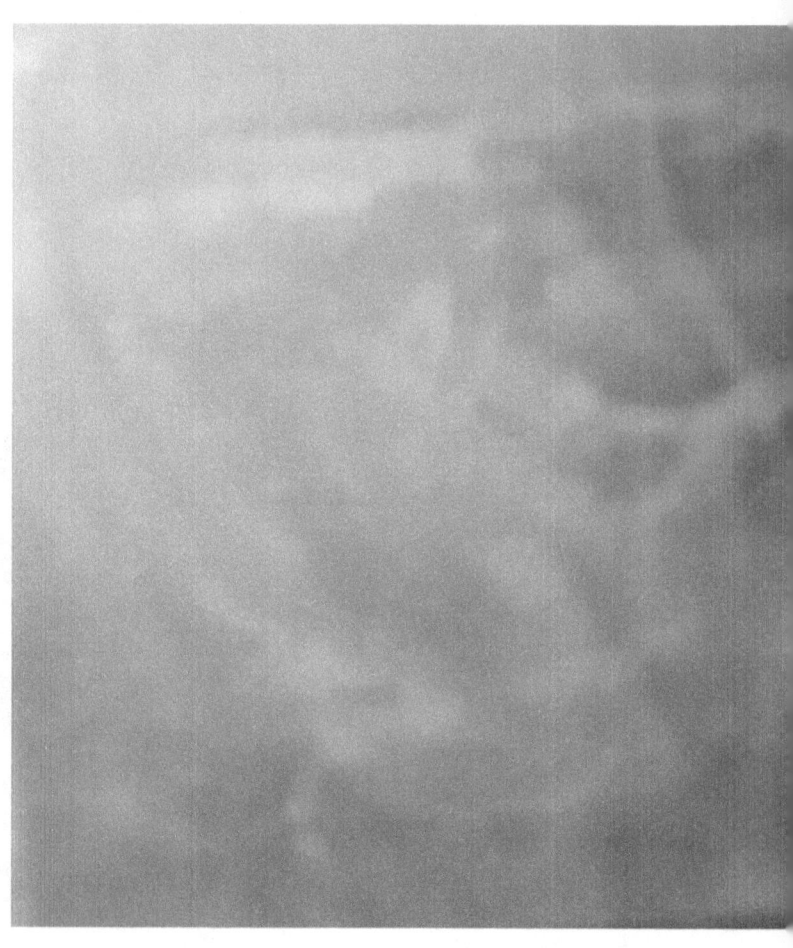

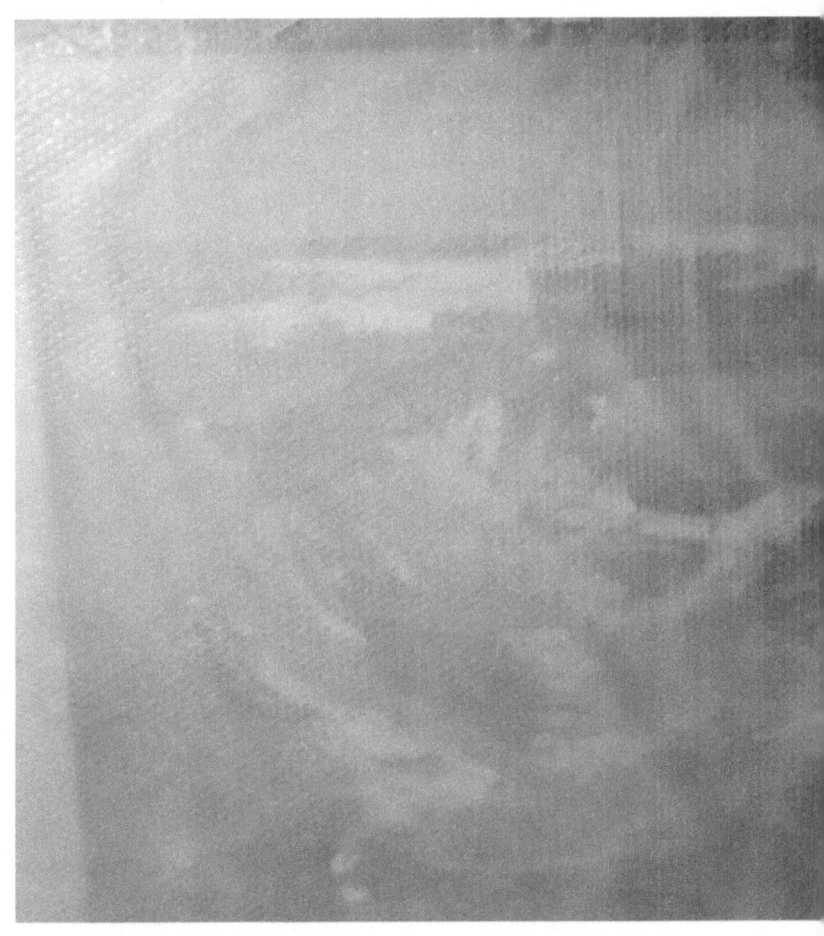

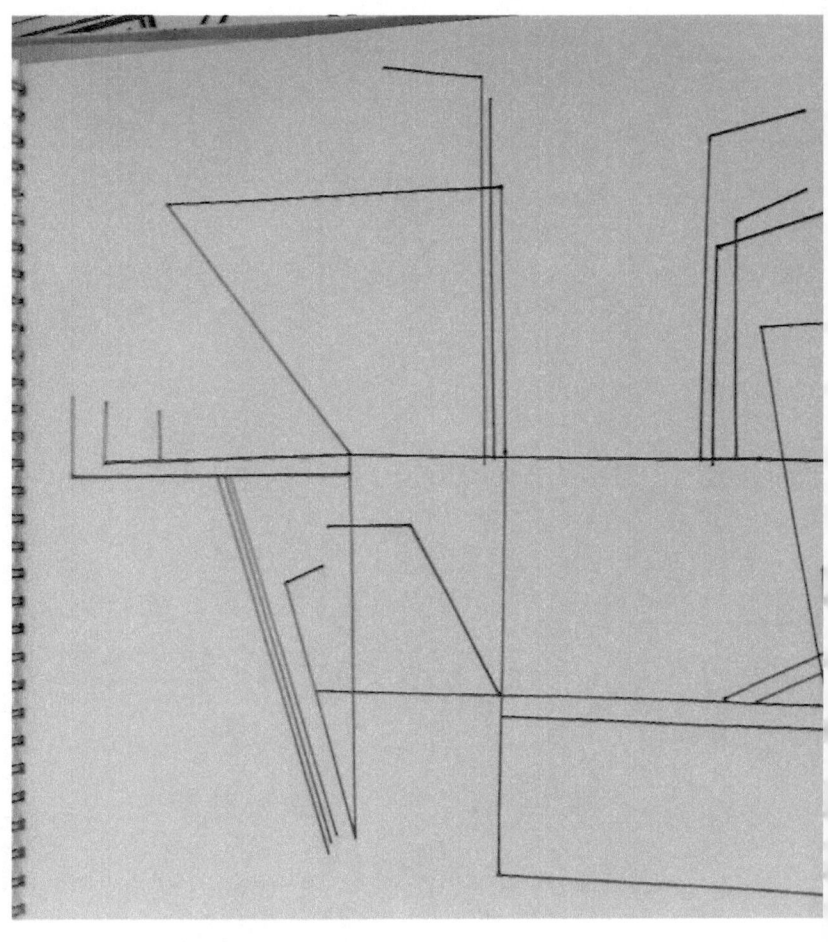

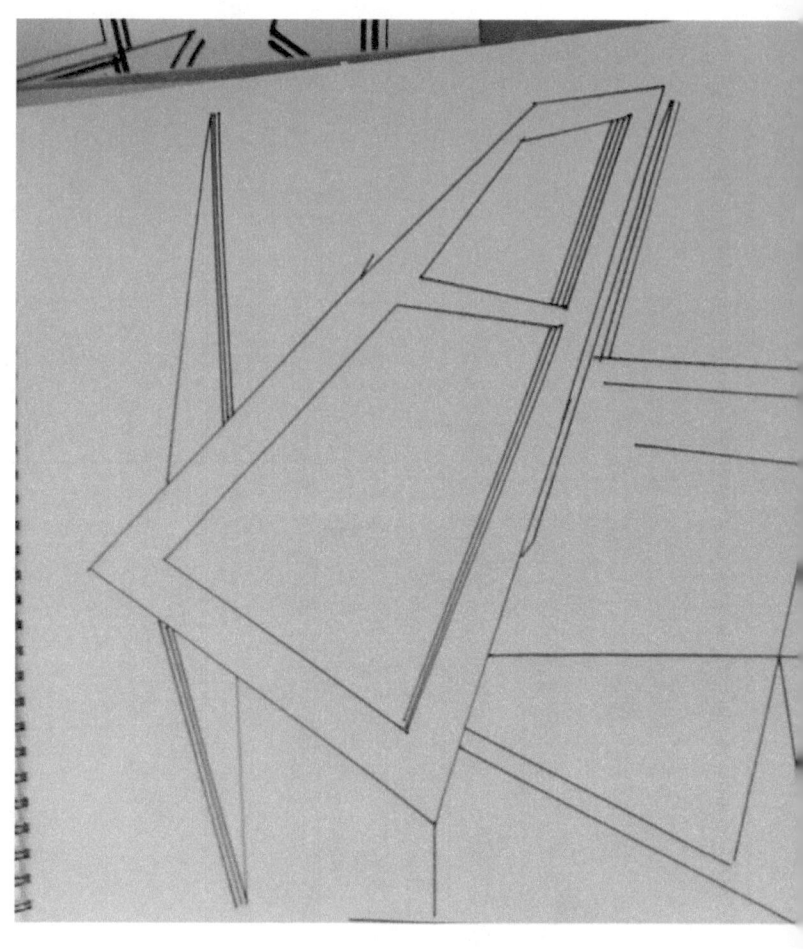

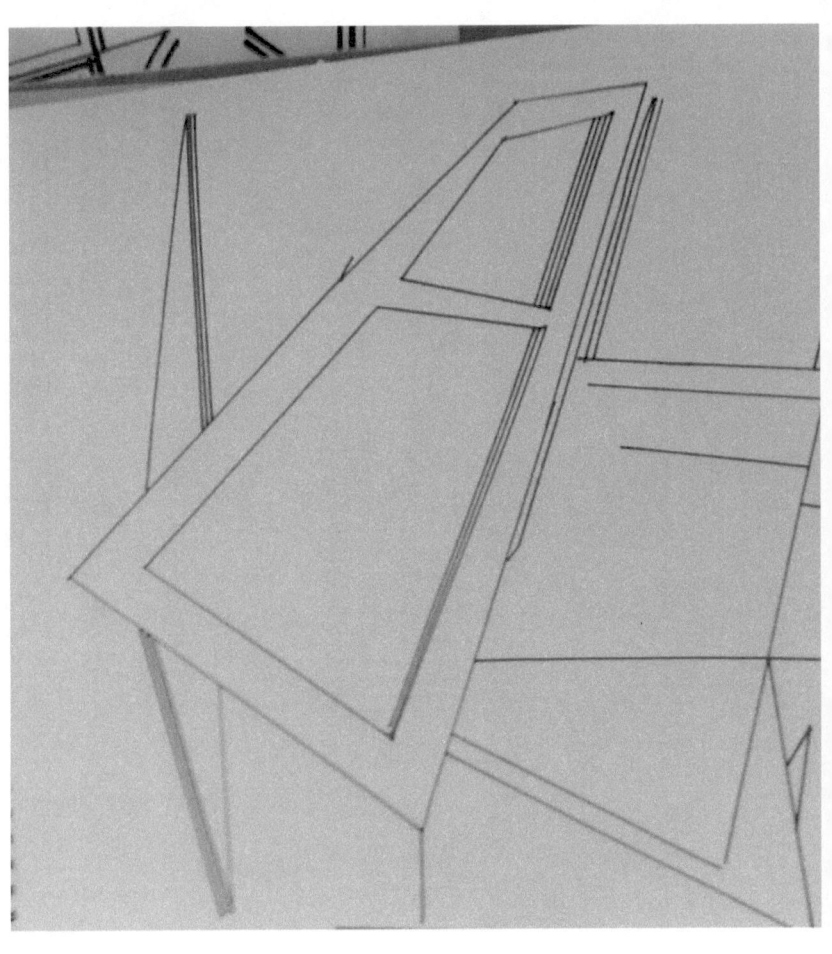

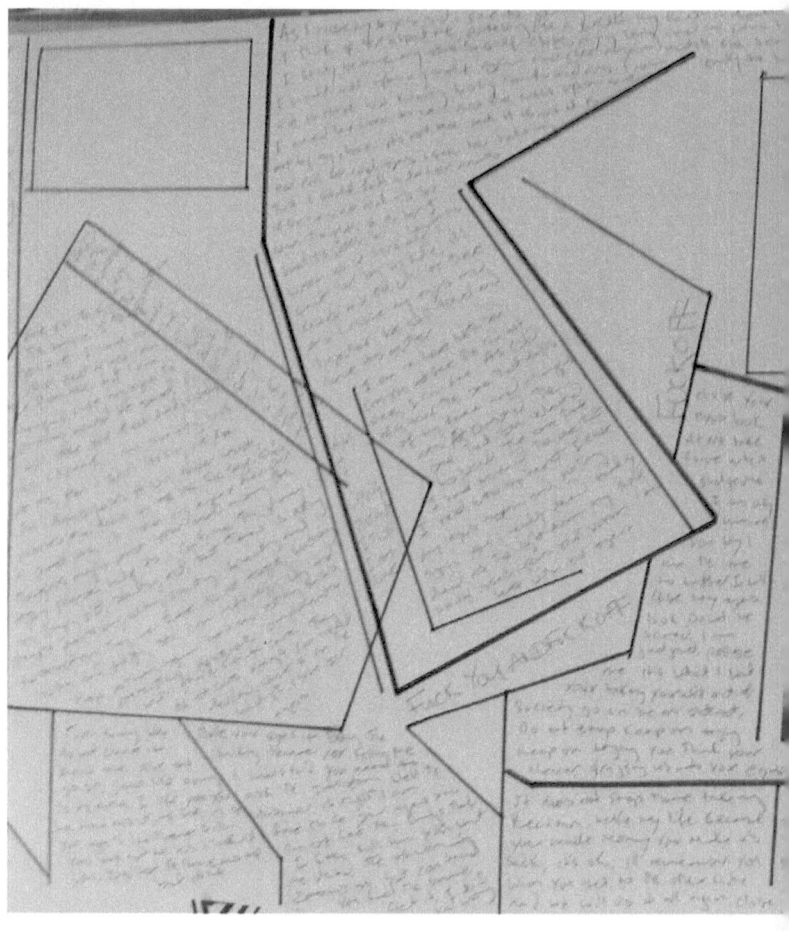

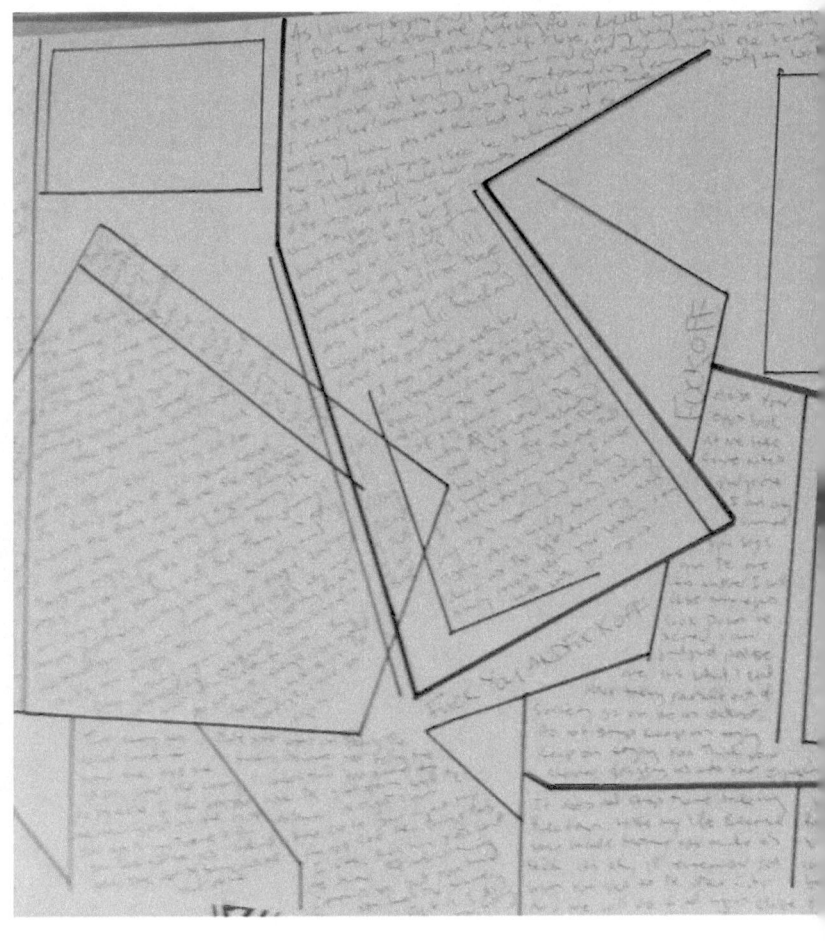

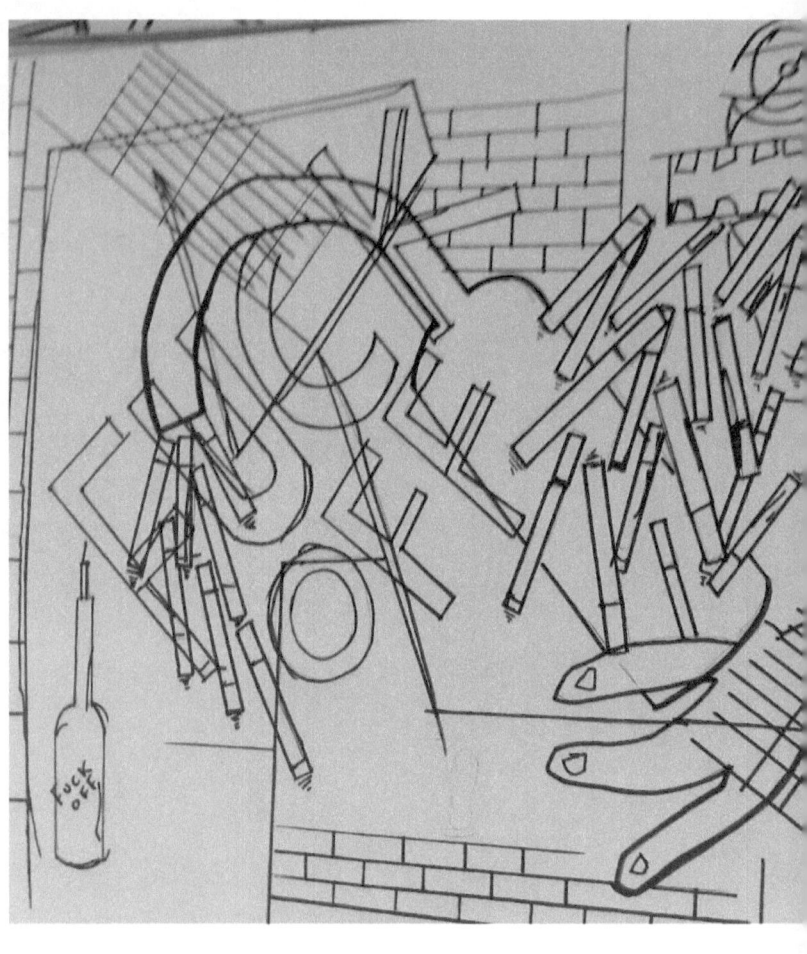

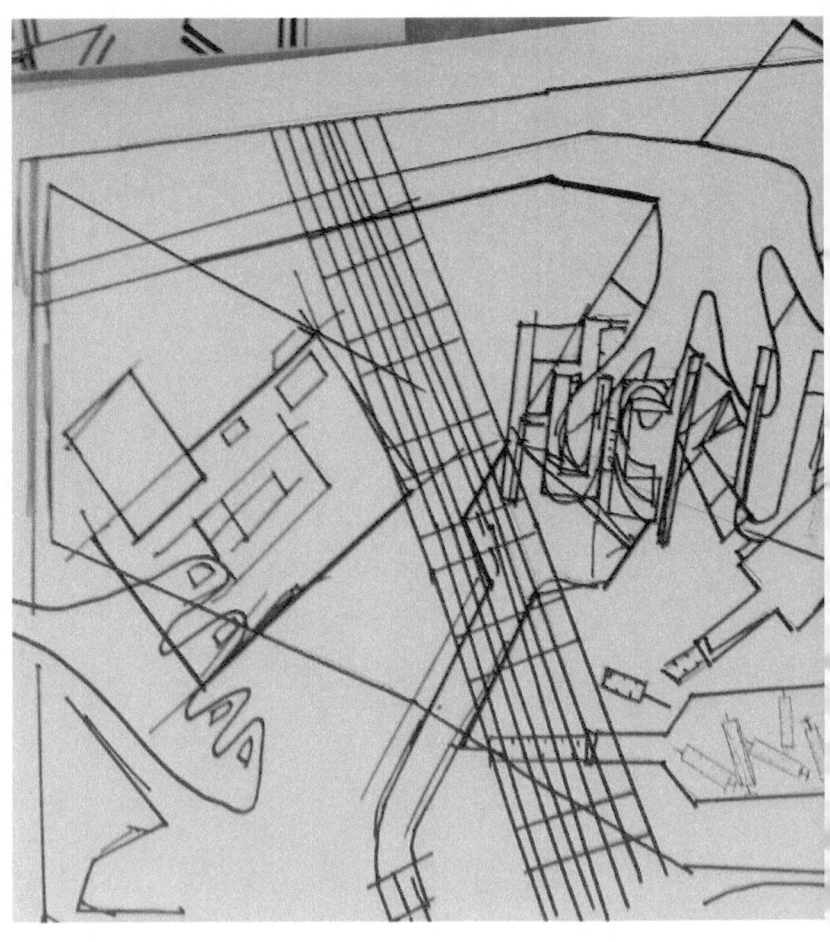

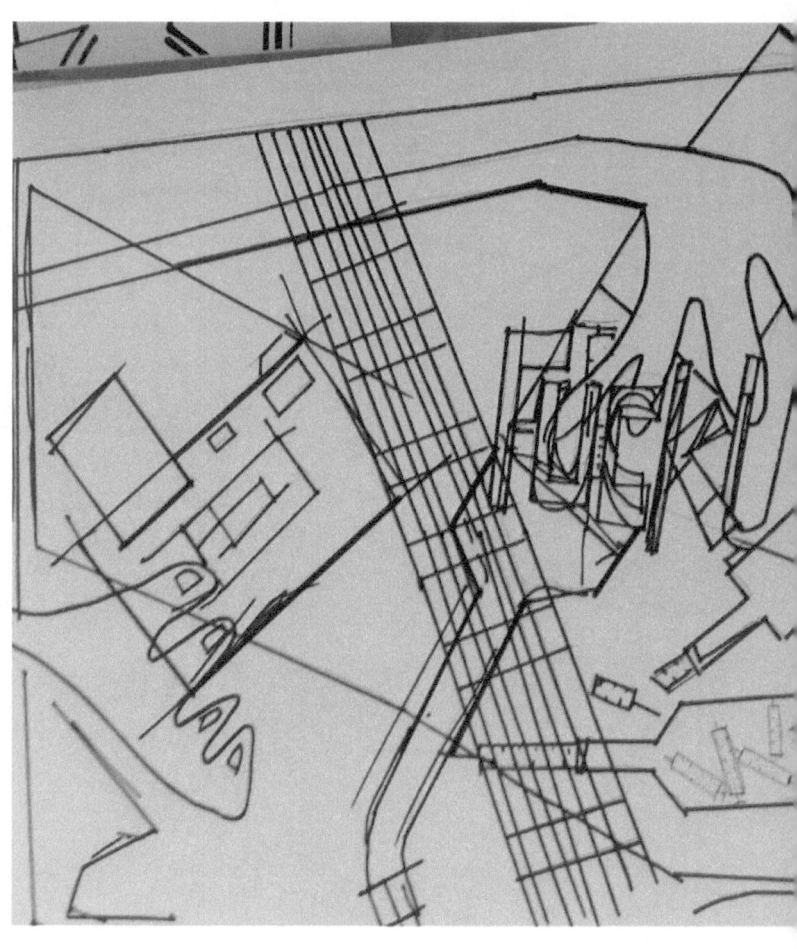

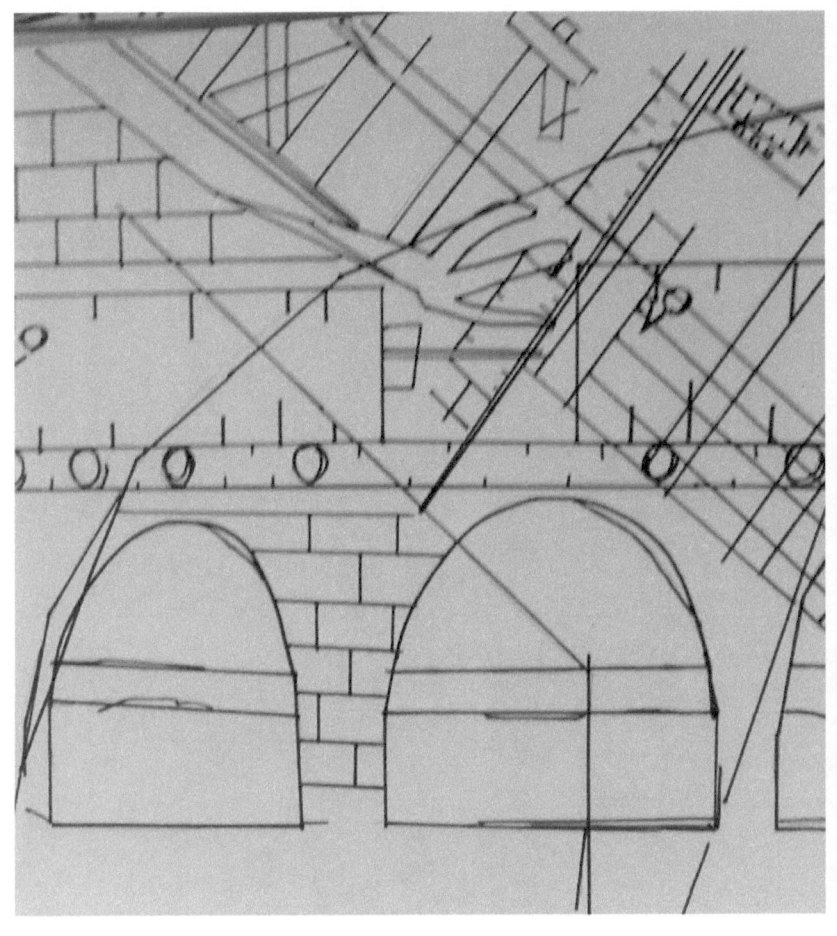

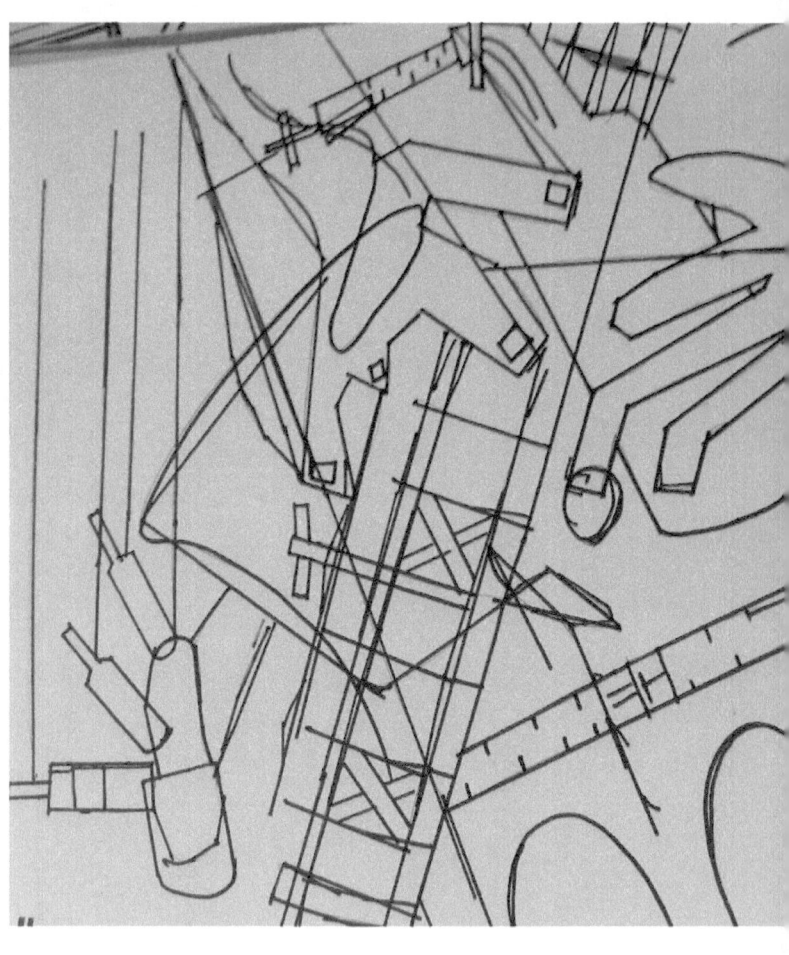

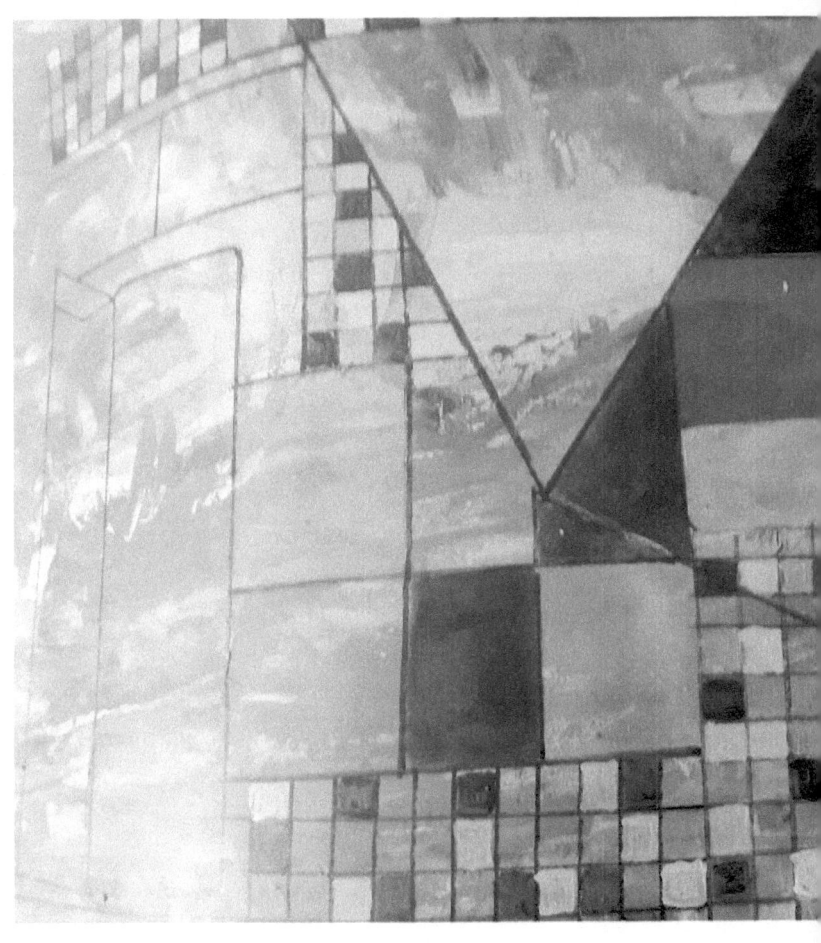

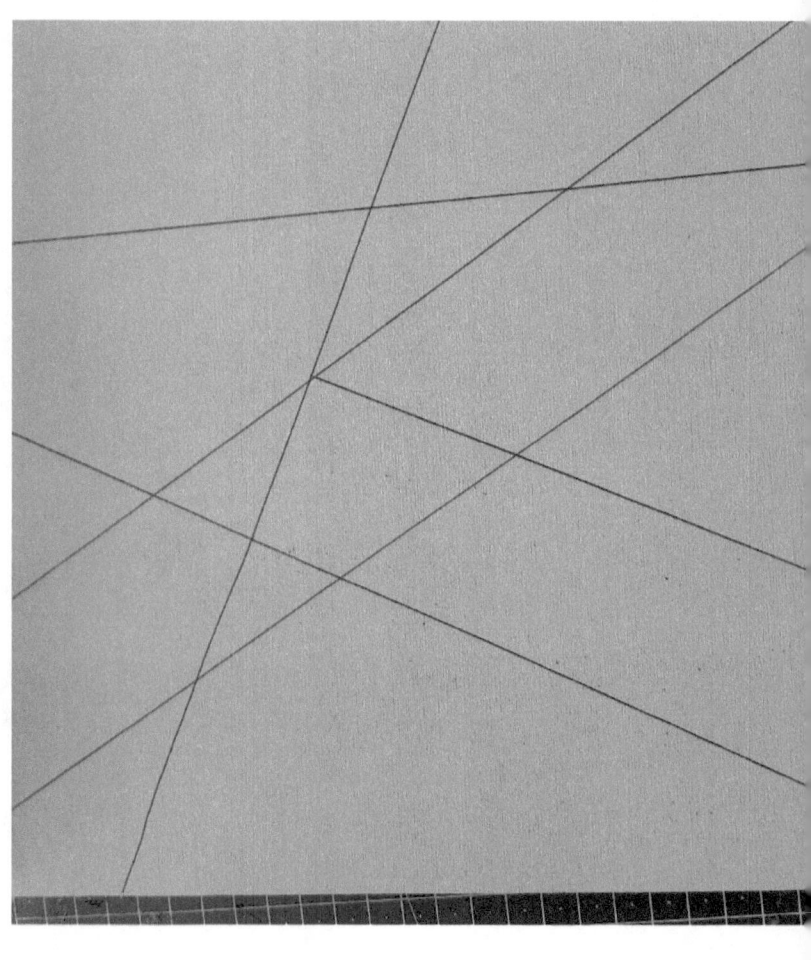

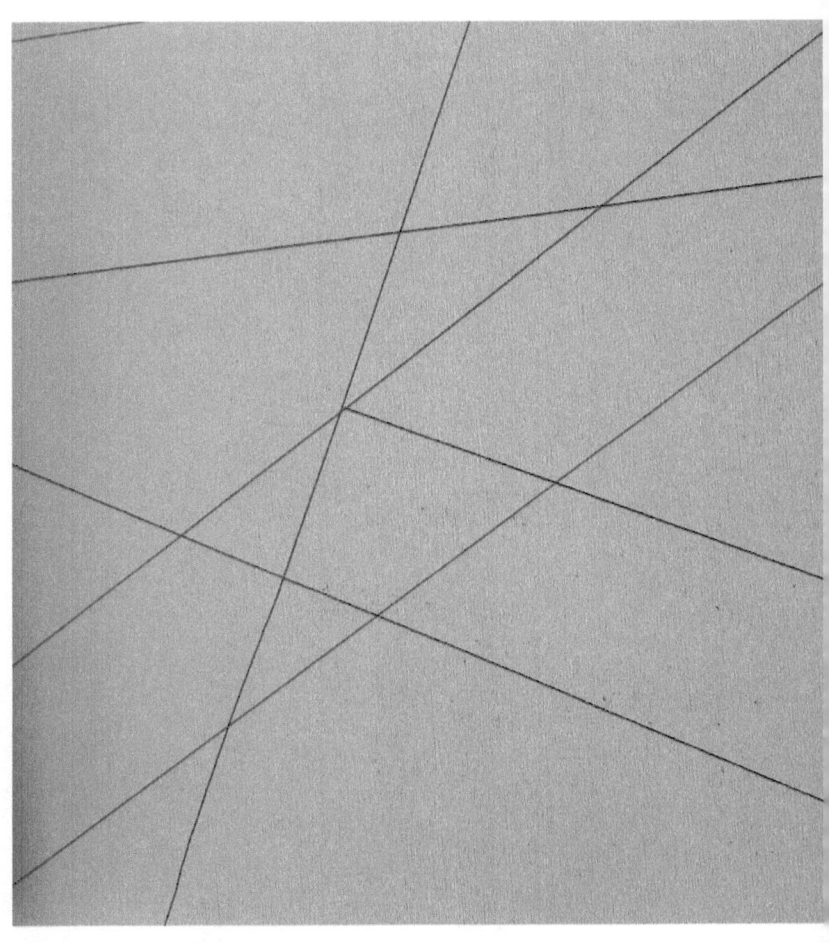

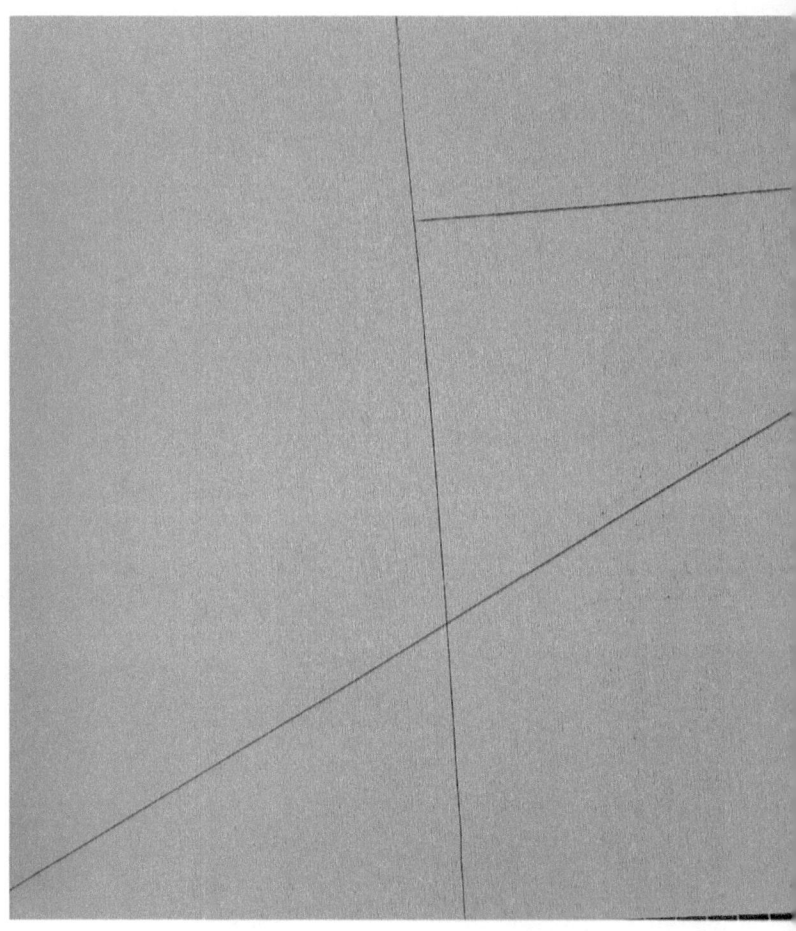

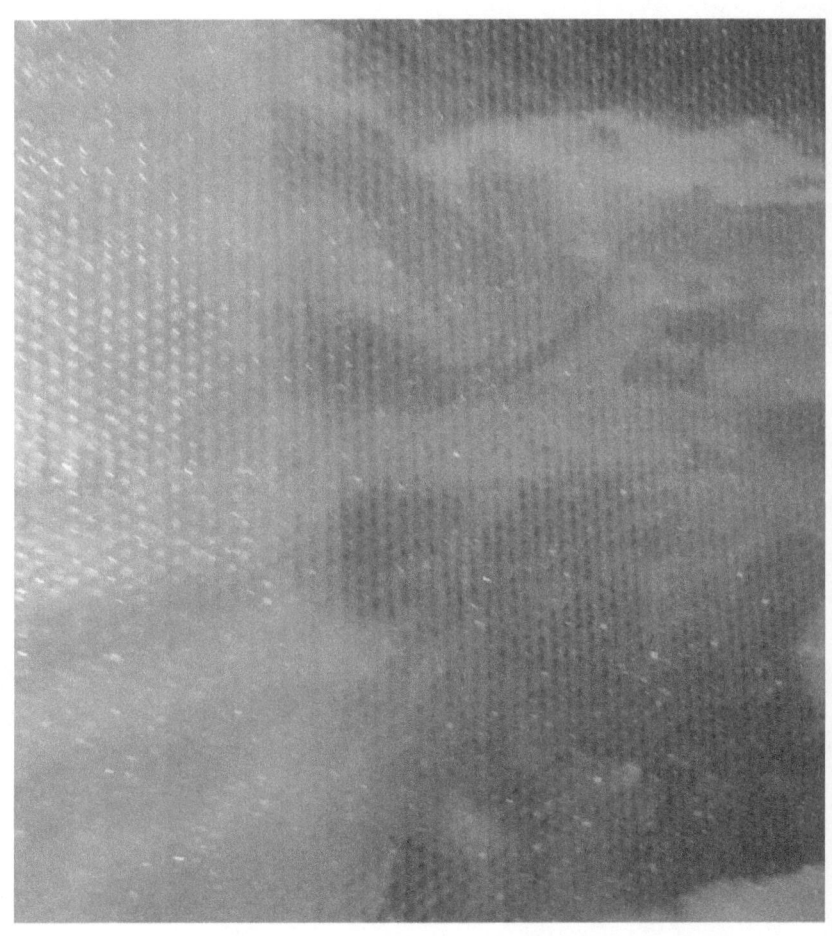

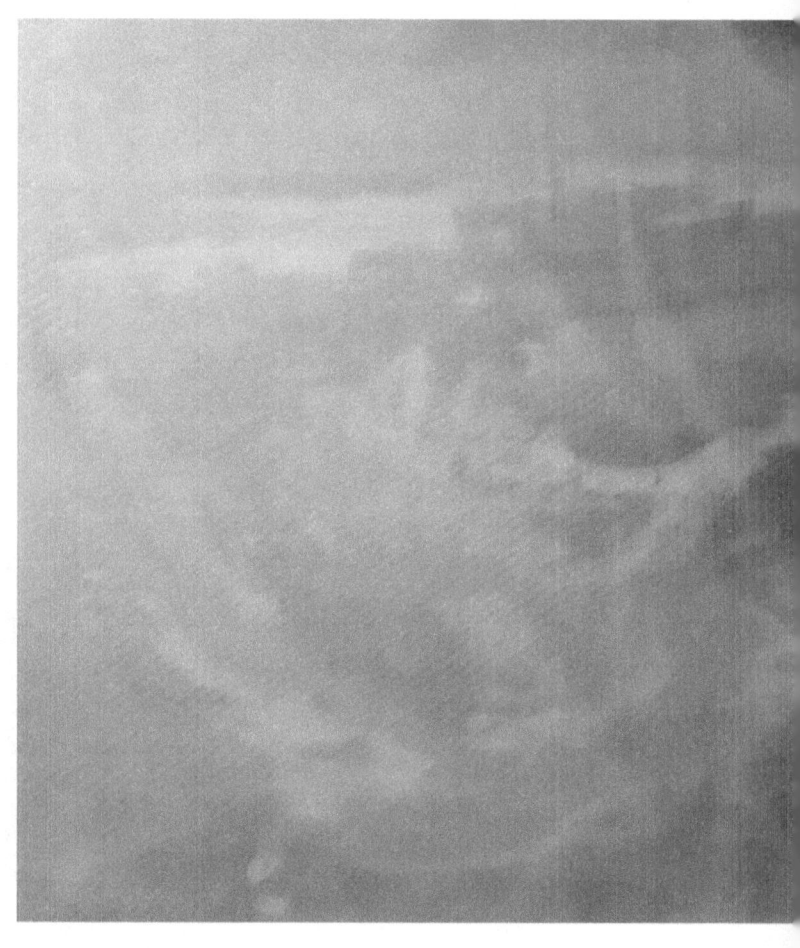

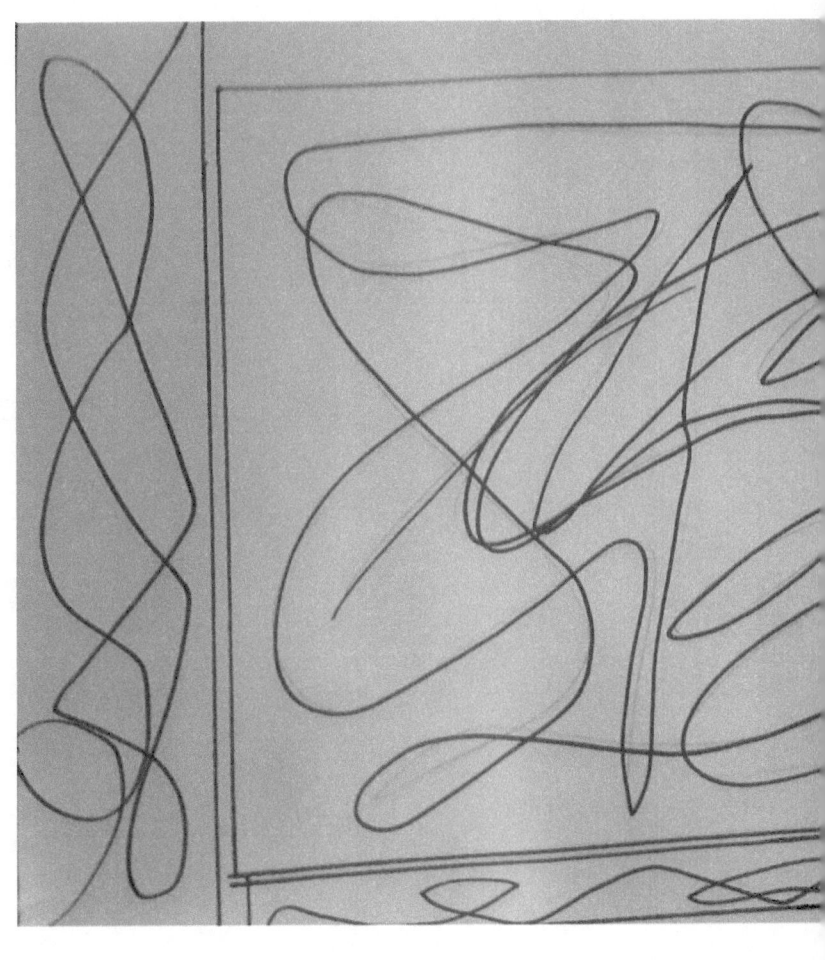

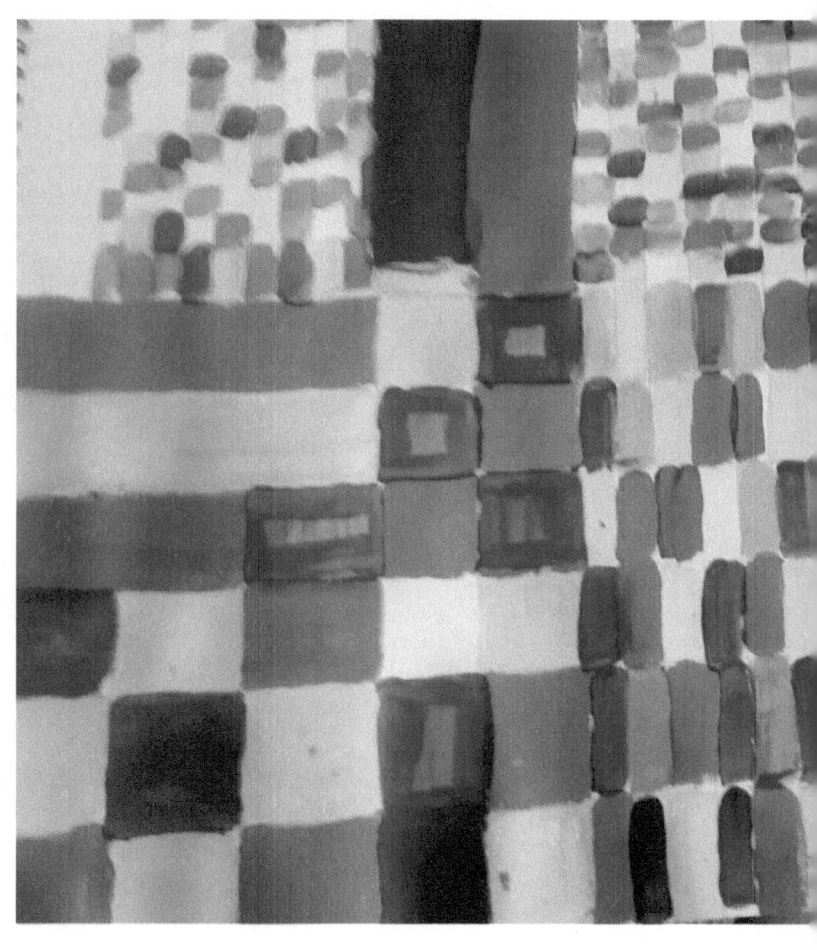

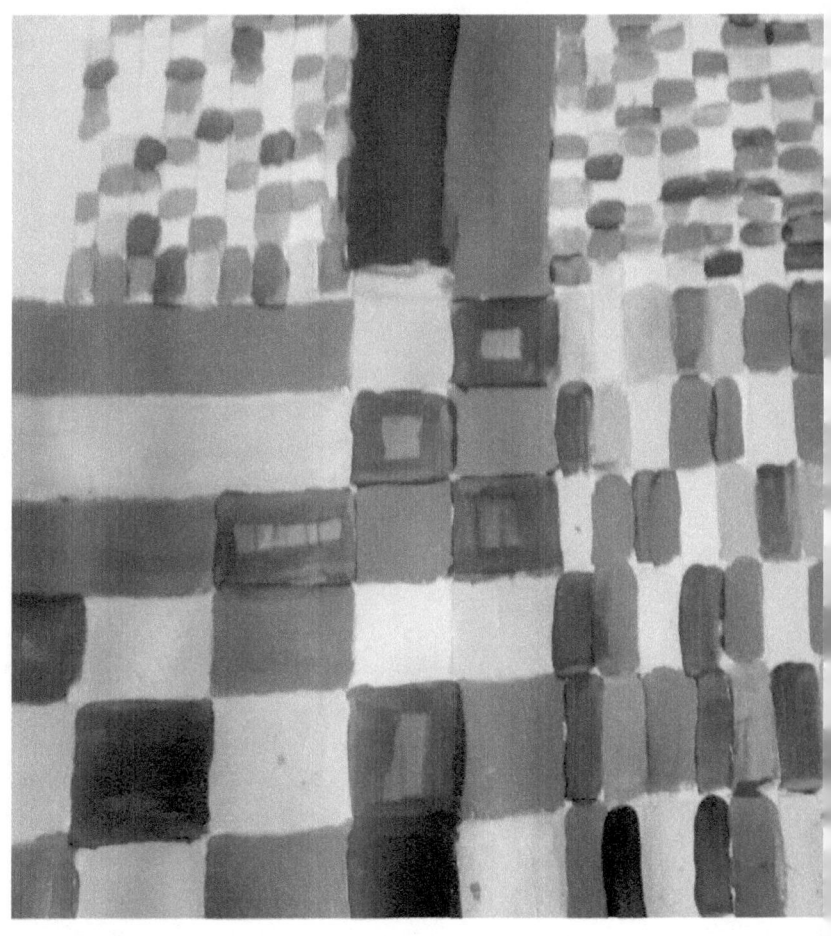

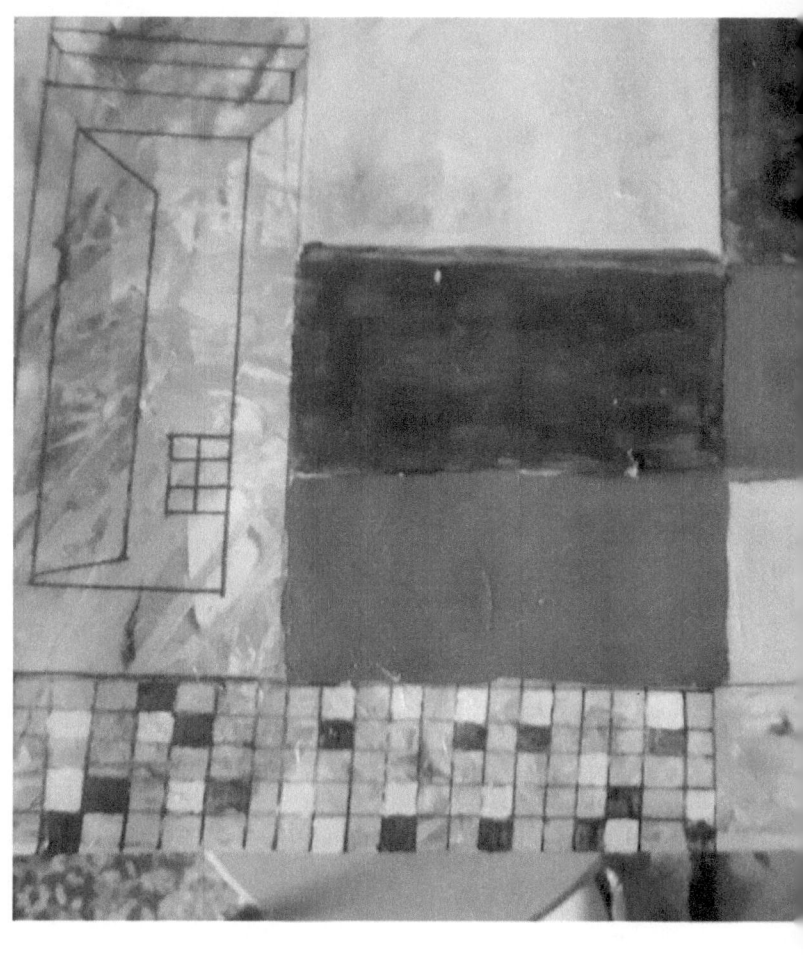

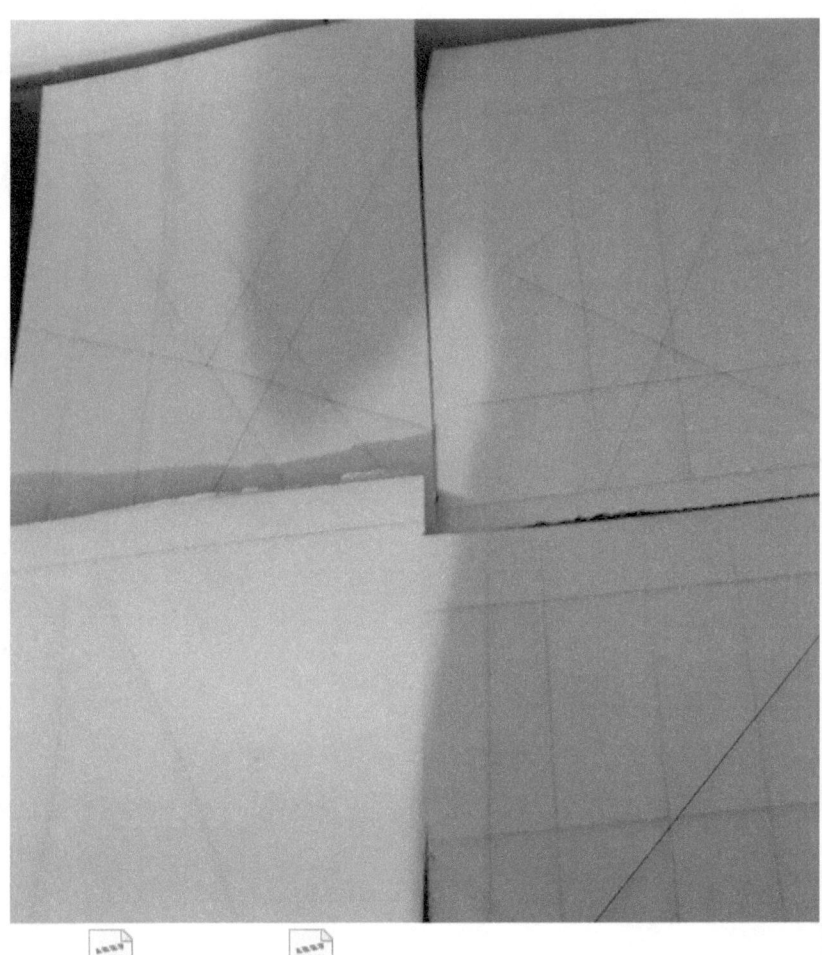

20200907_171336.mp4   20200907_171333.mp4

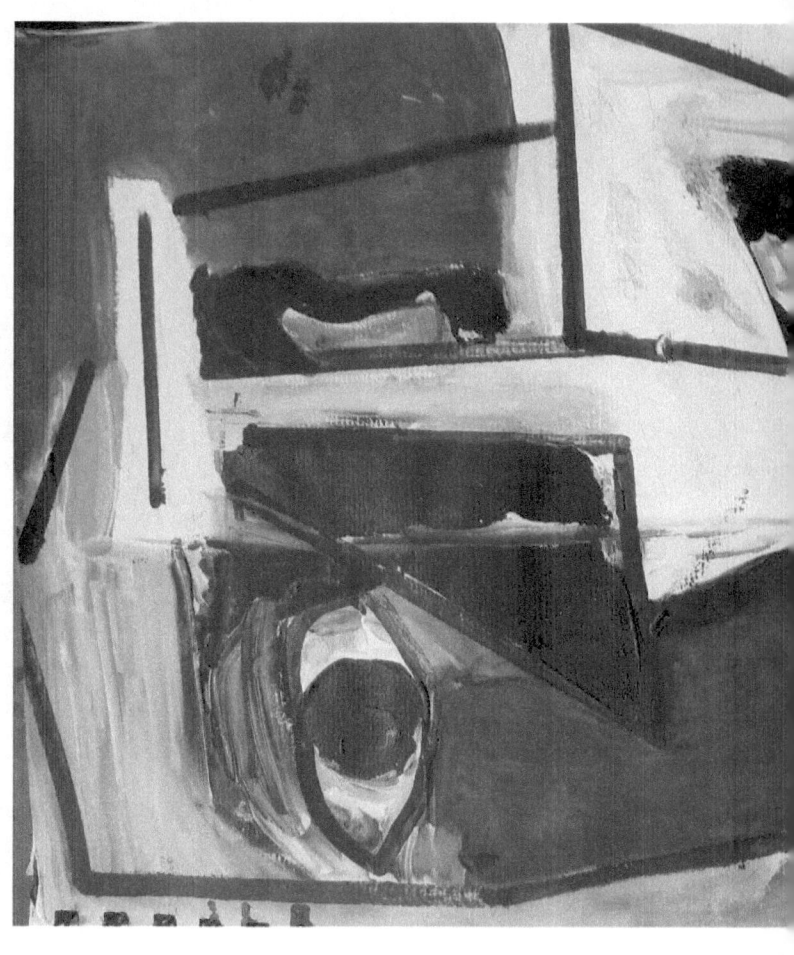

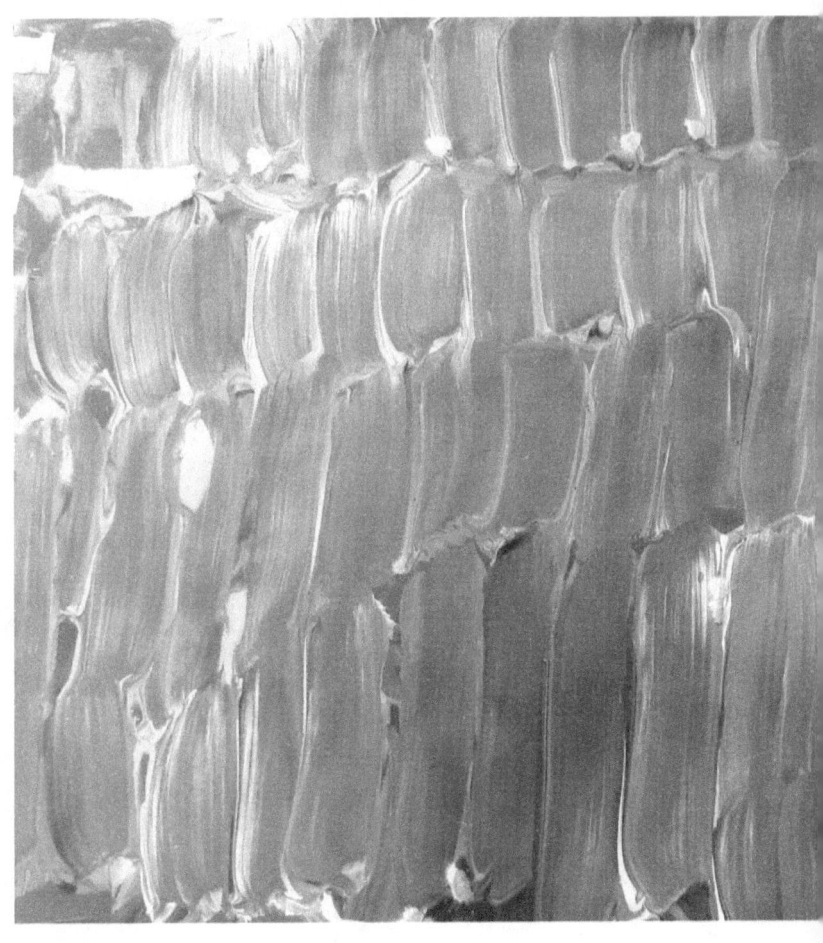

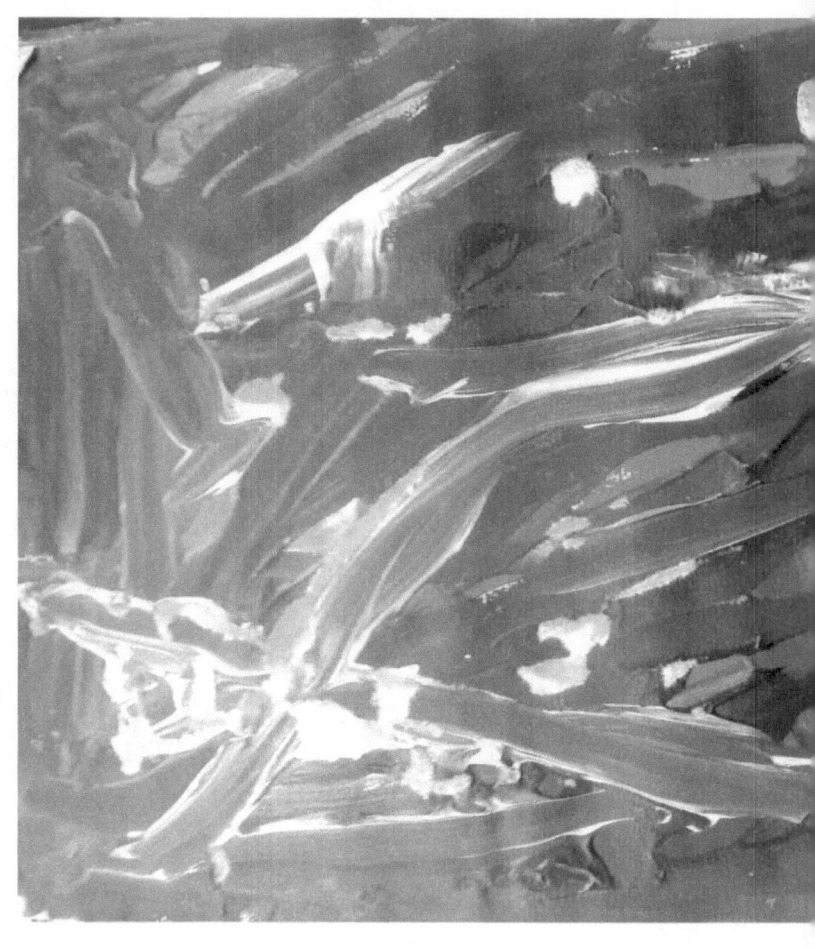

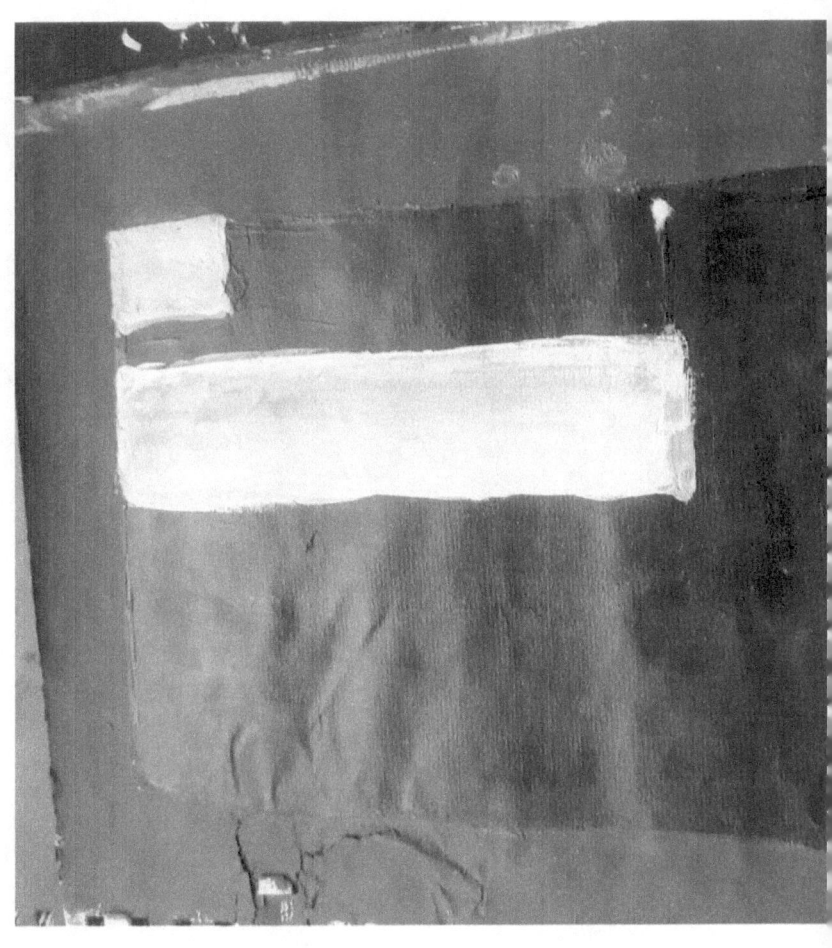

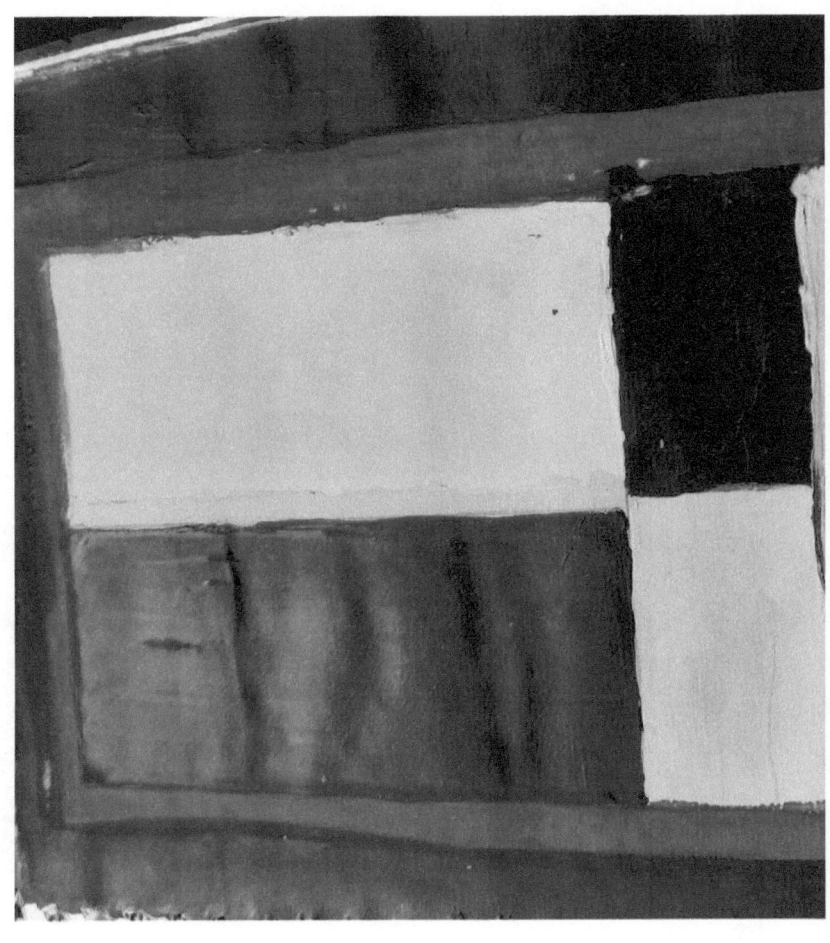

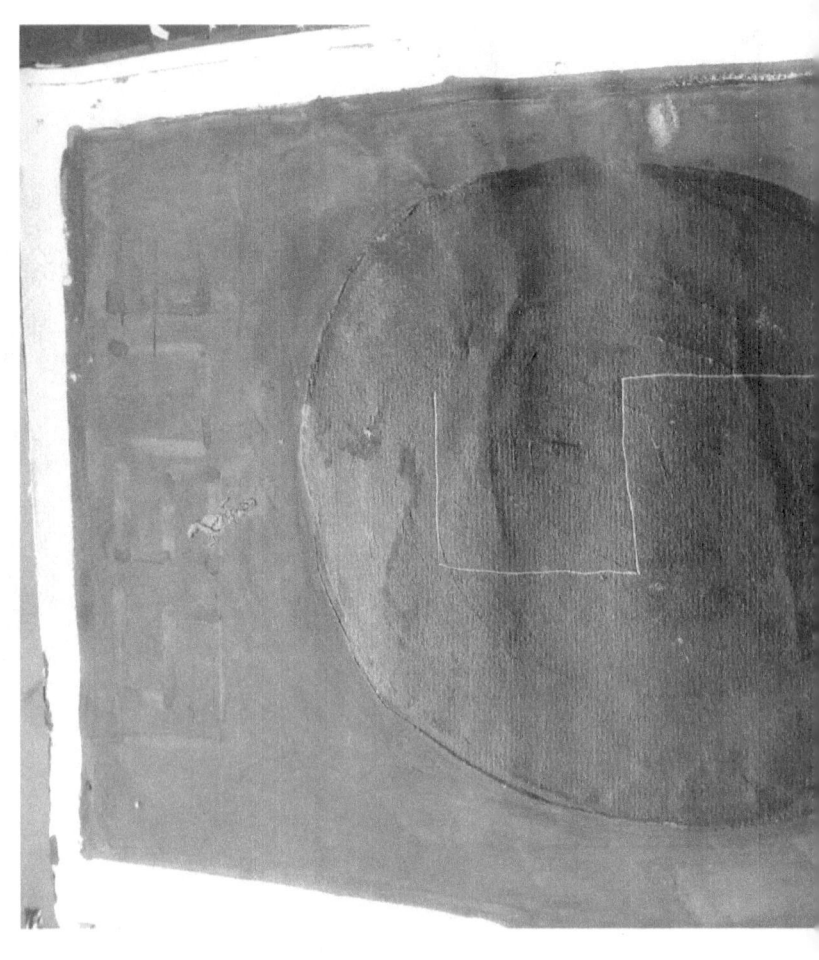

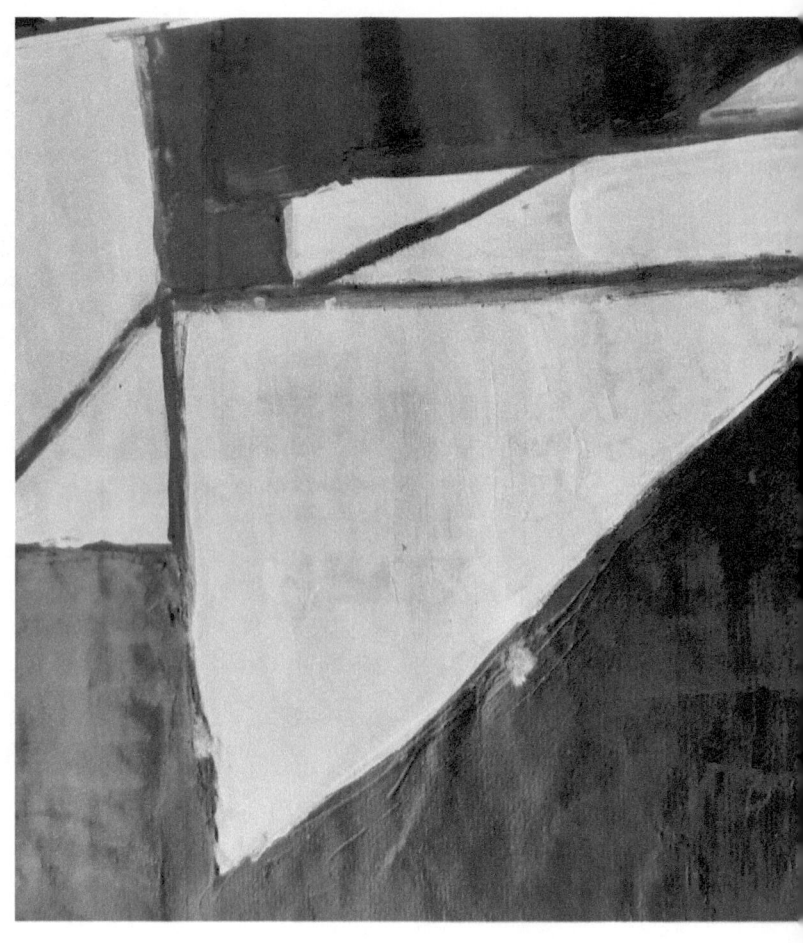

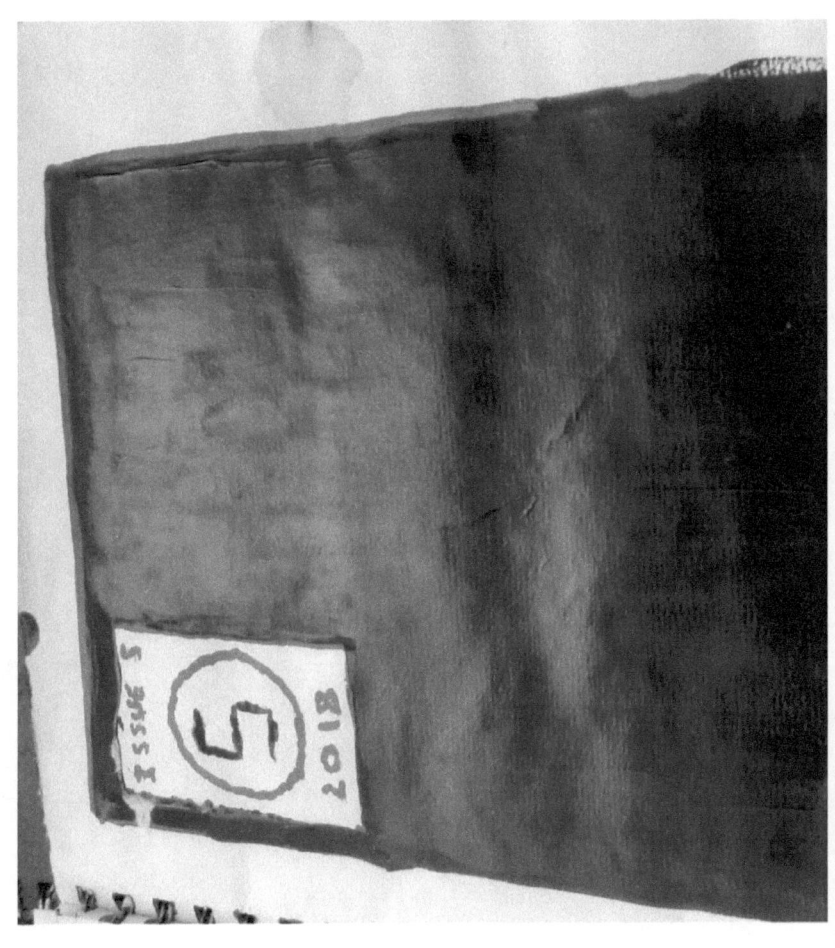

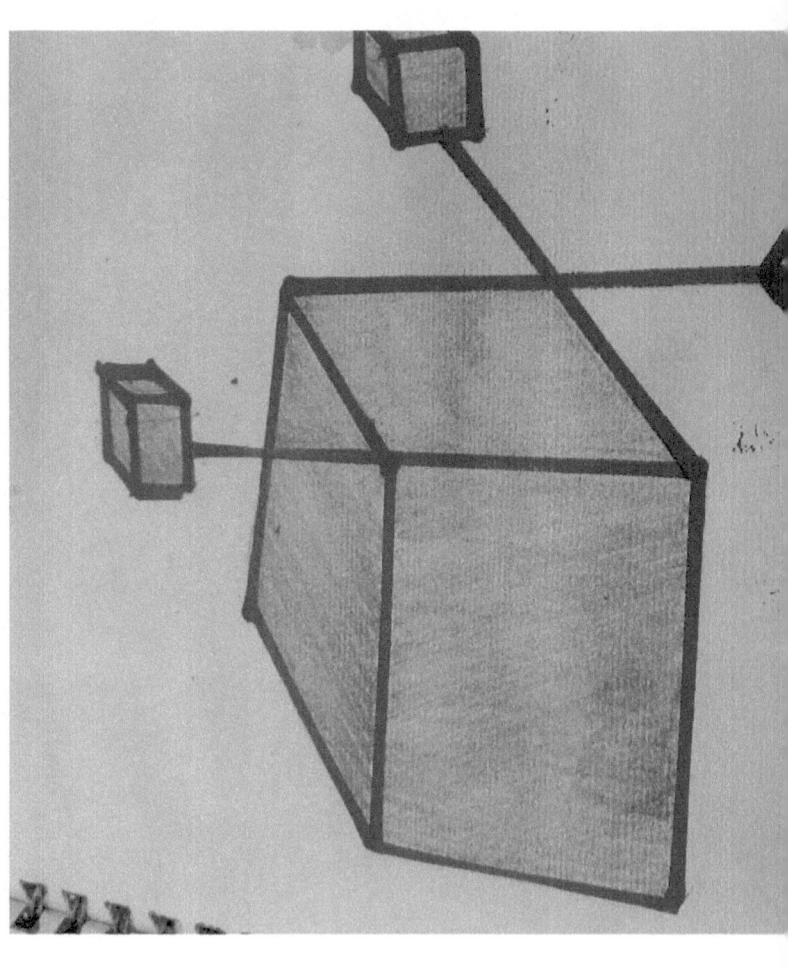

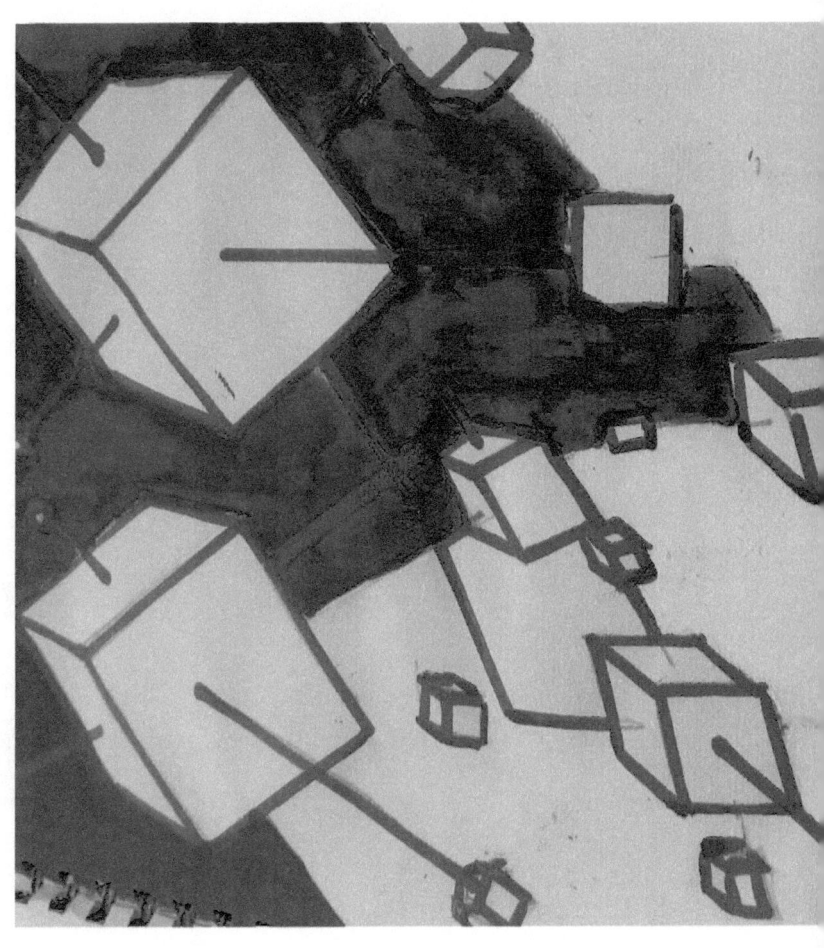

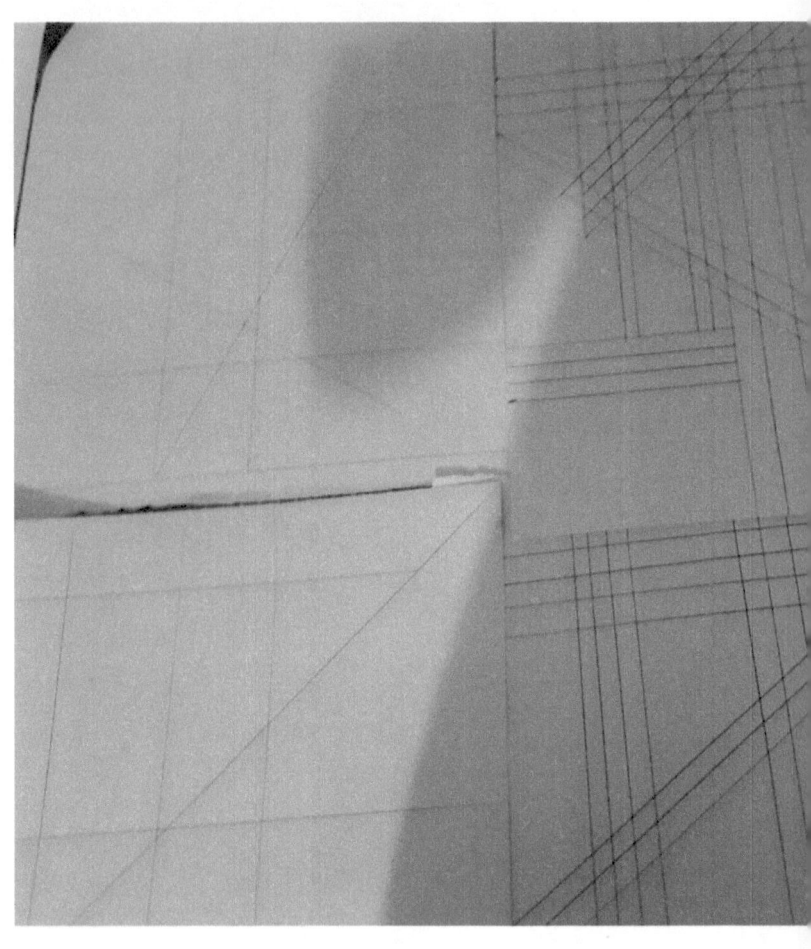

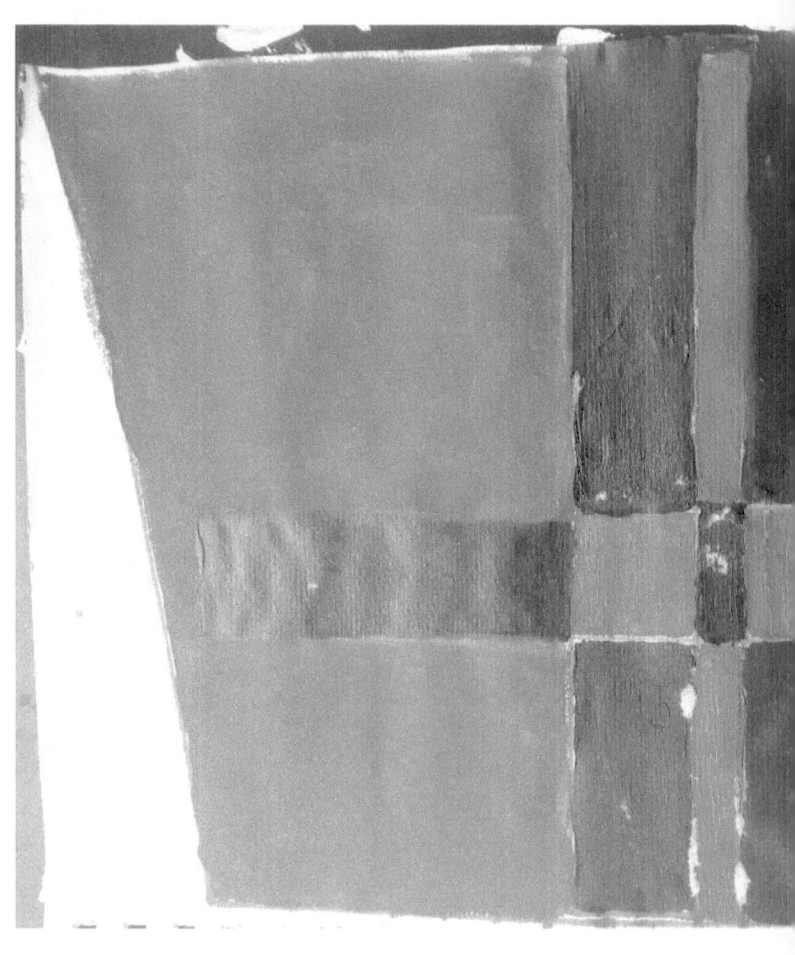

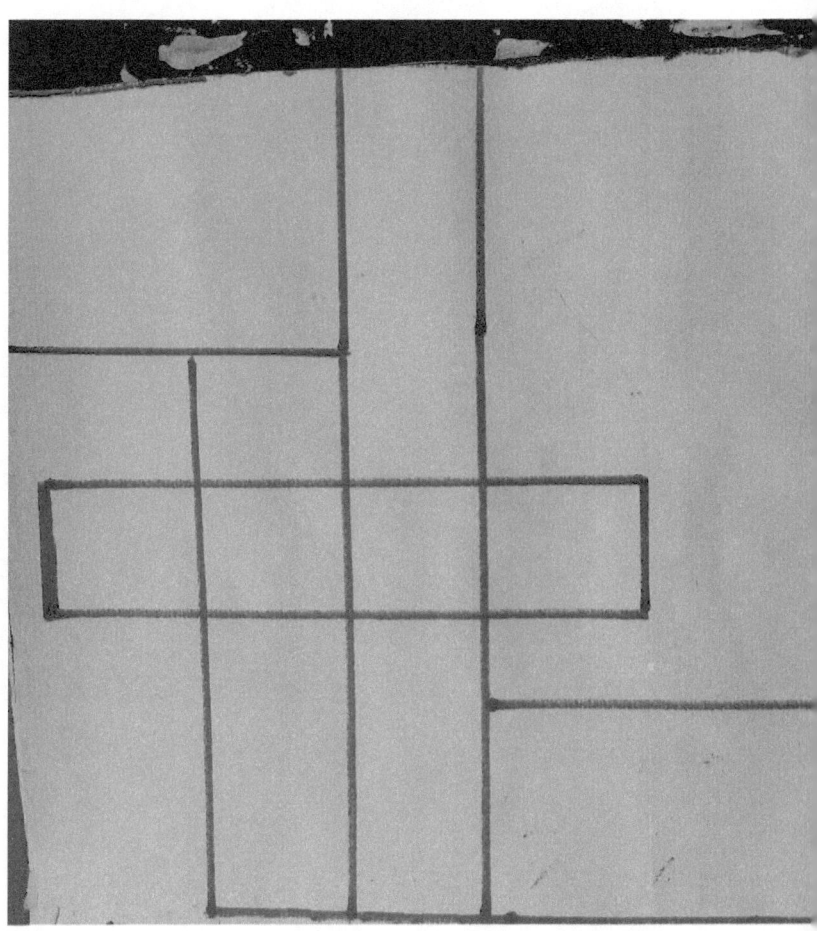

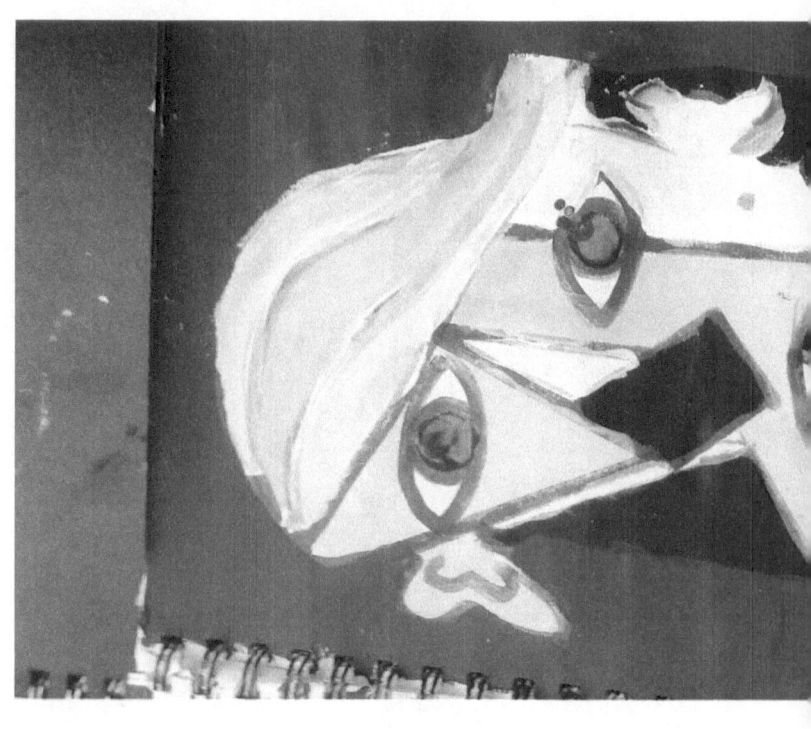

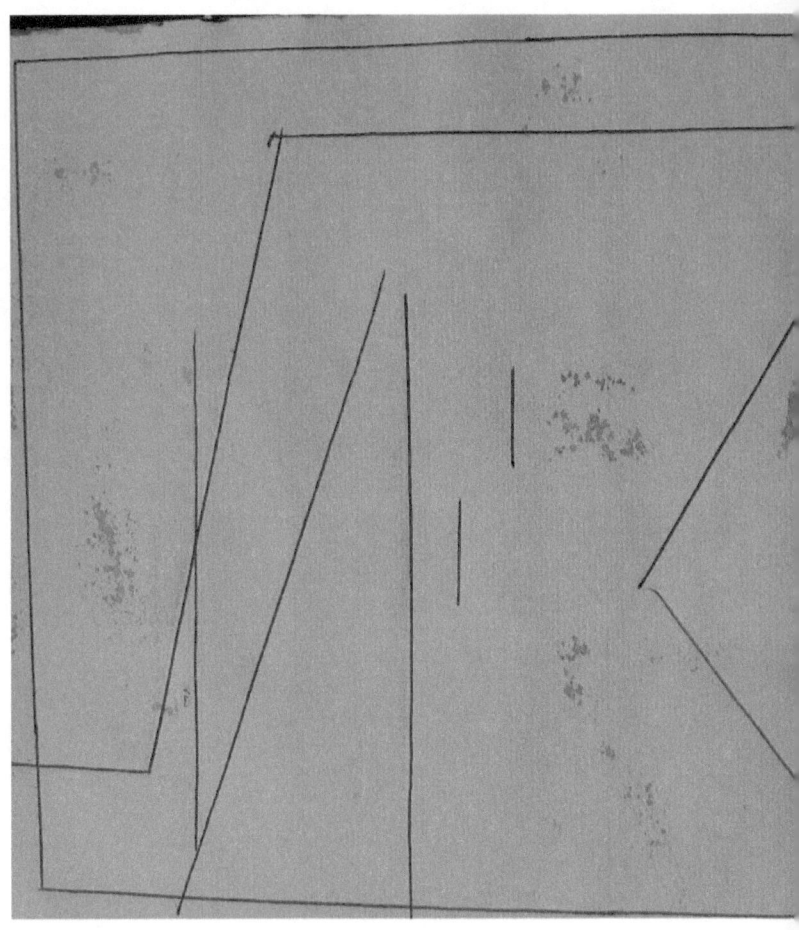

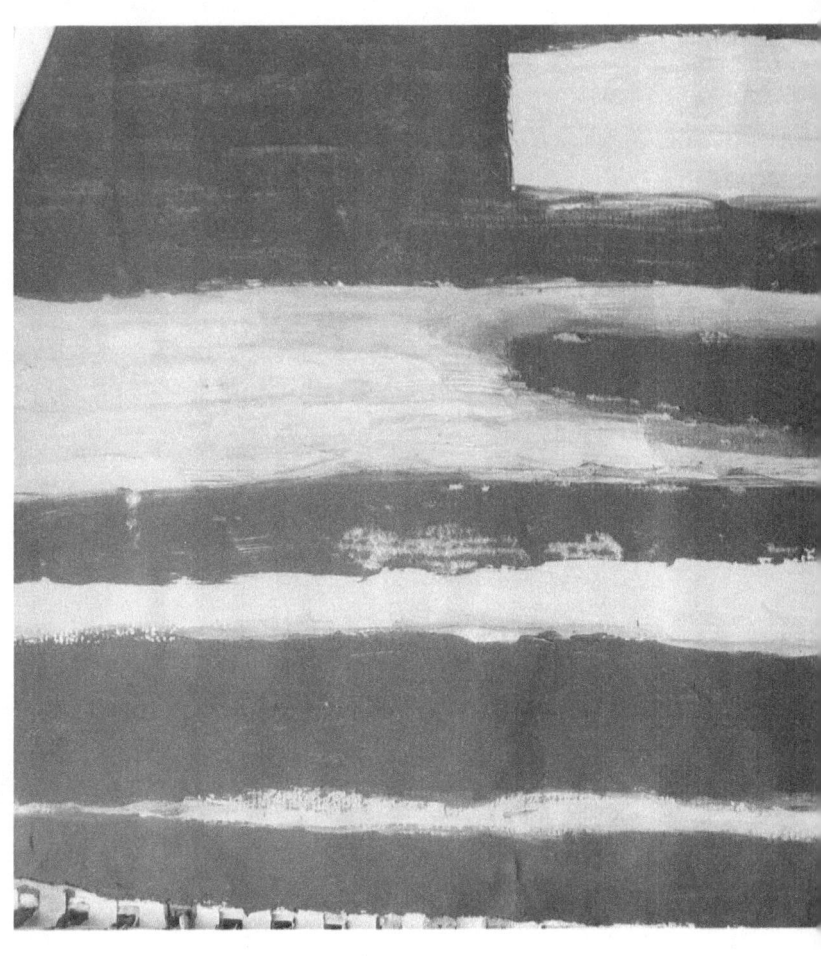

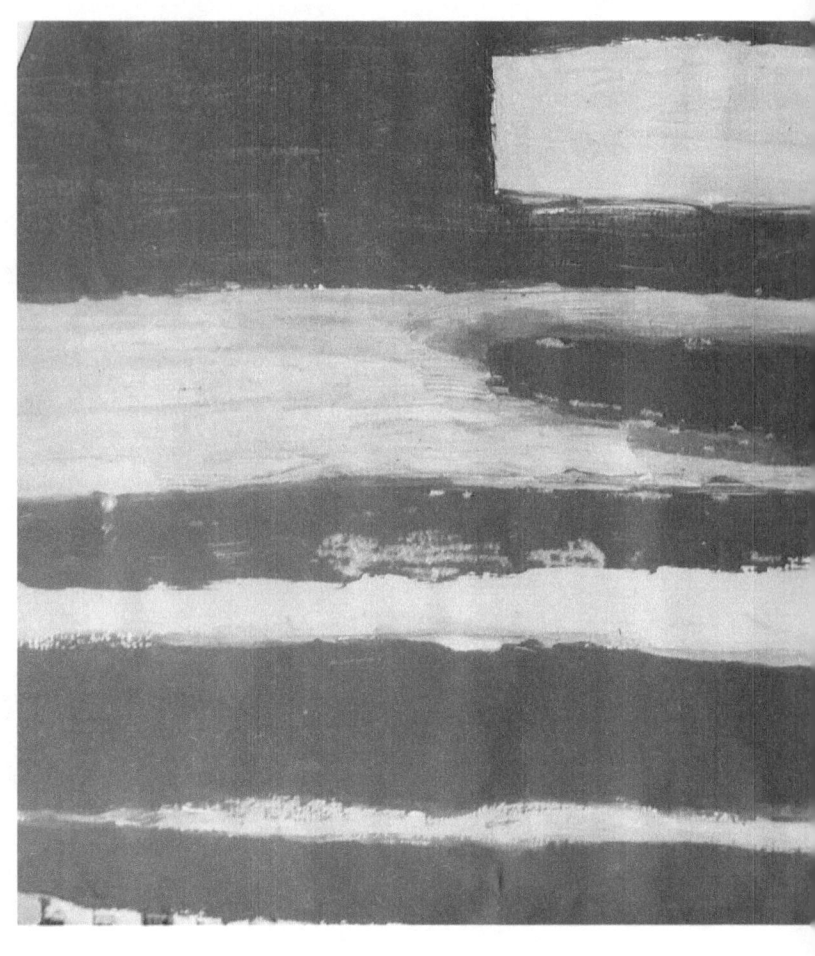

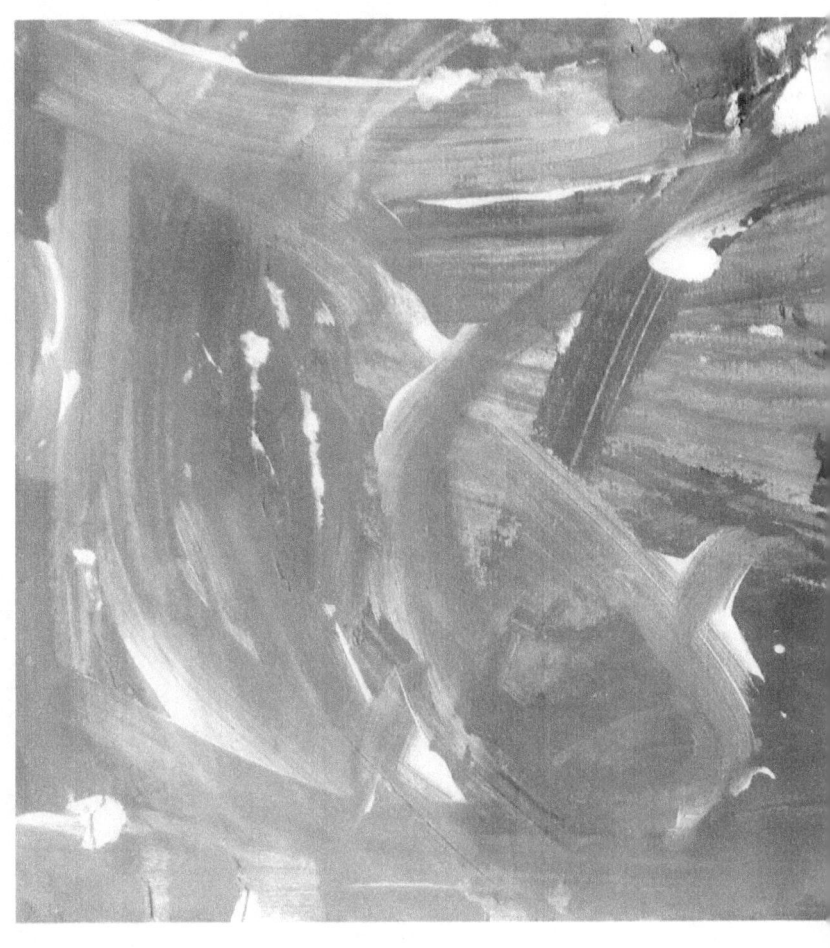

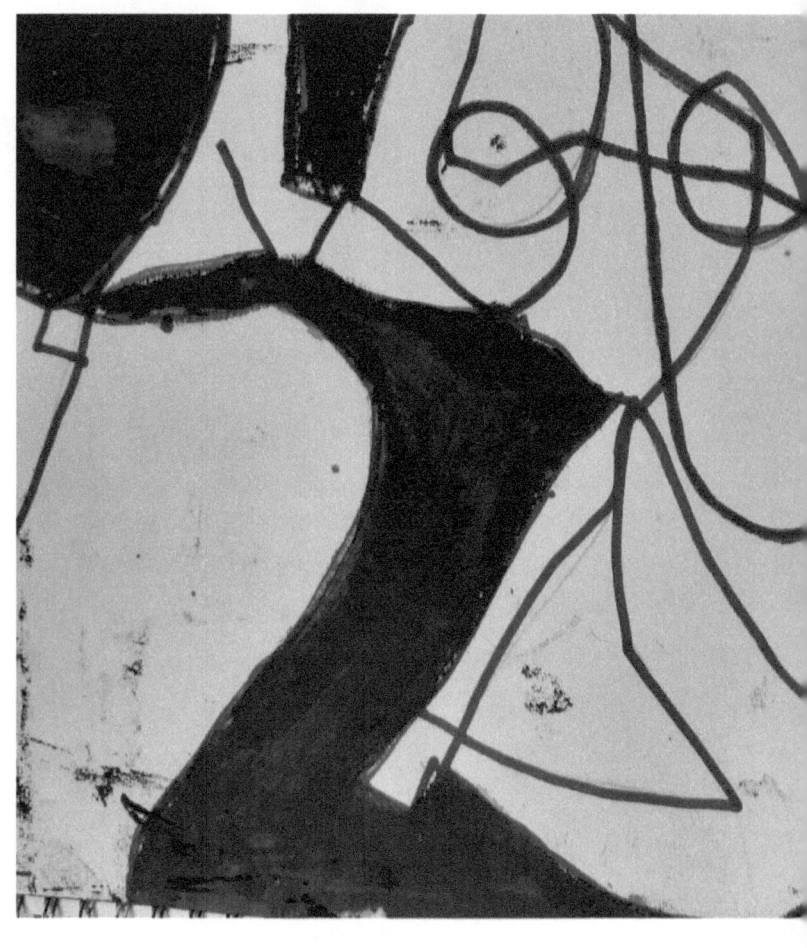

20200907_171342.mp4

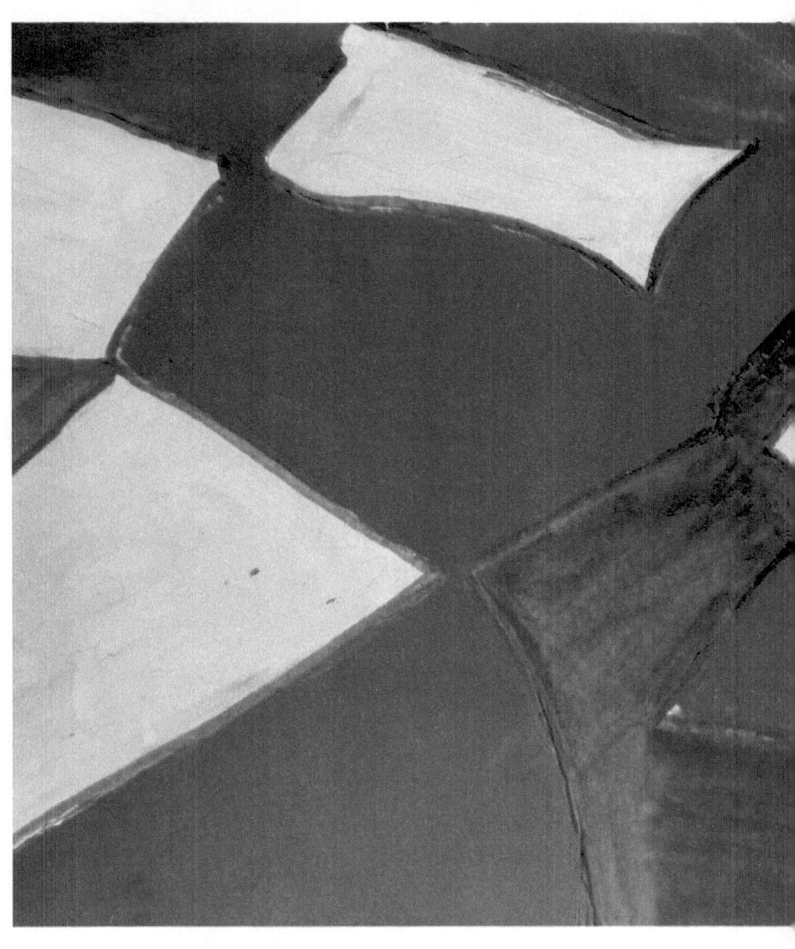

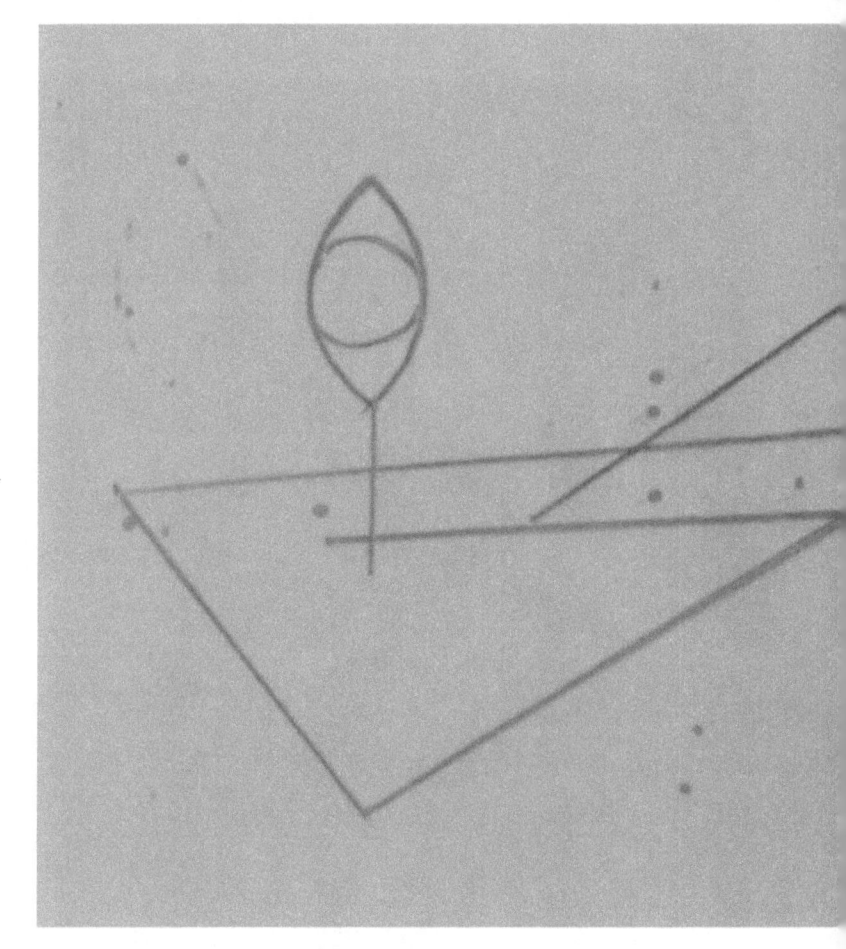

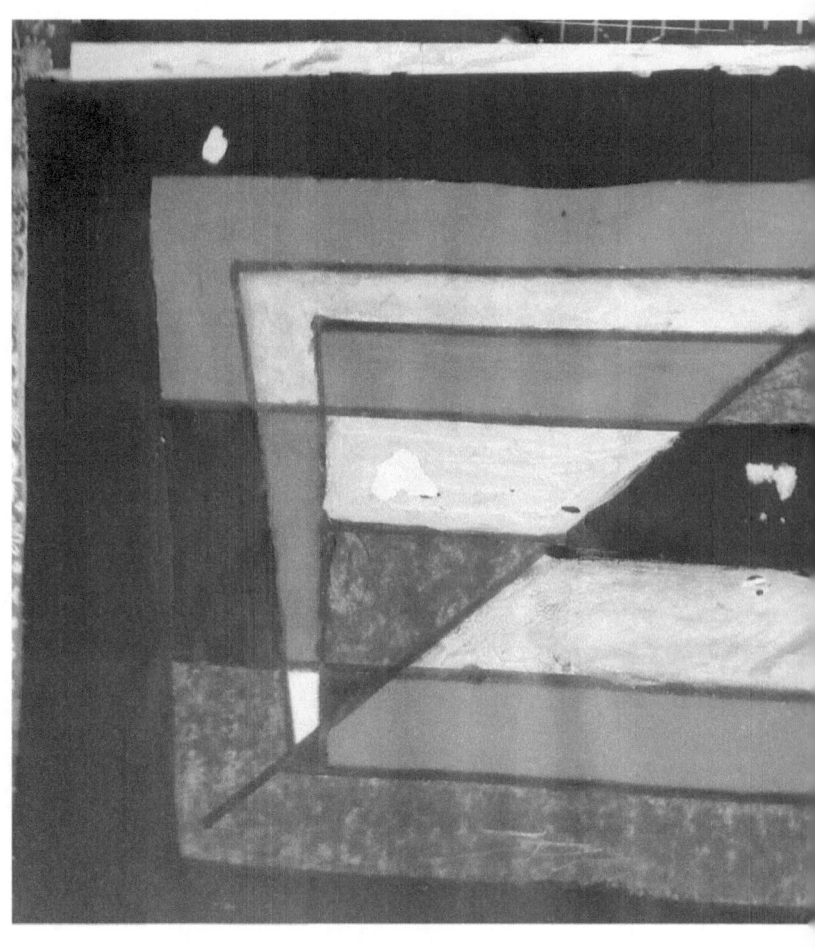

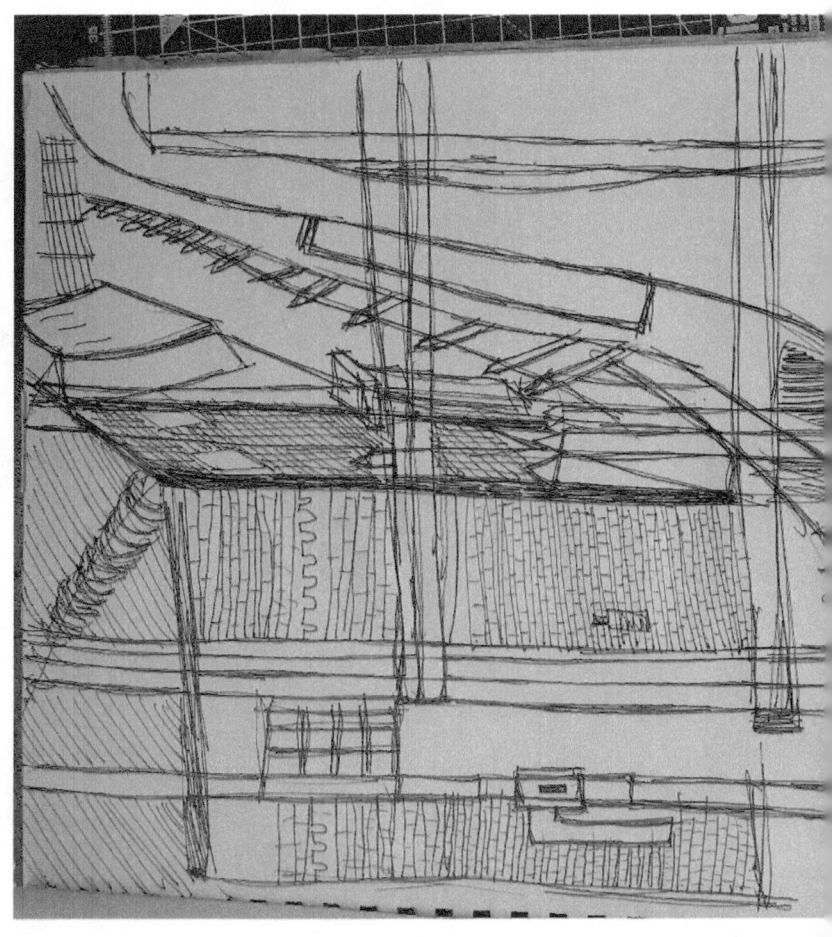

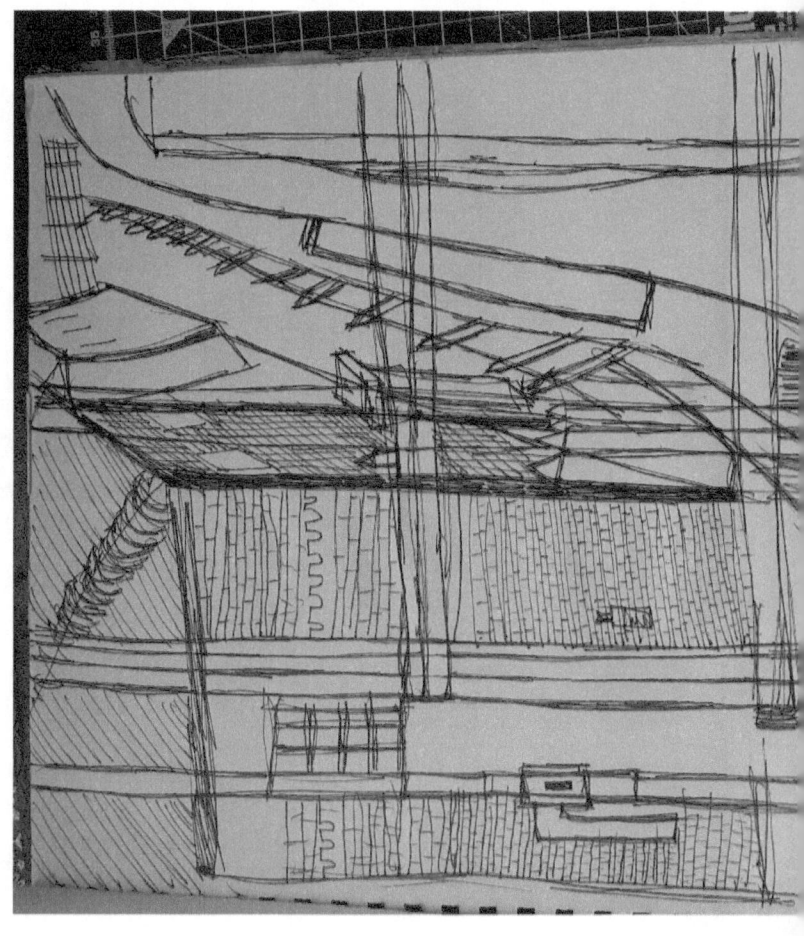

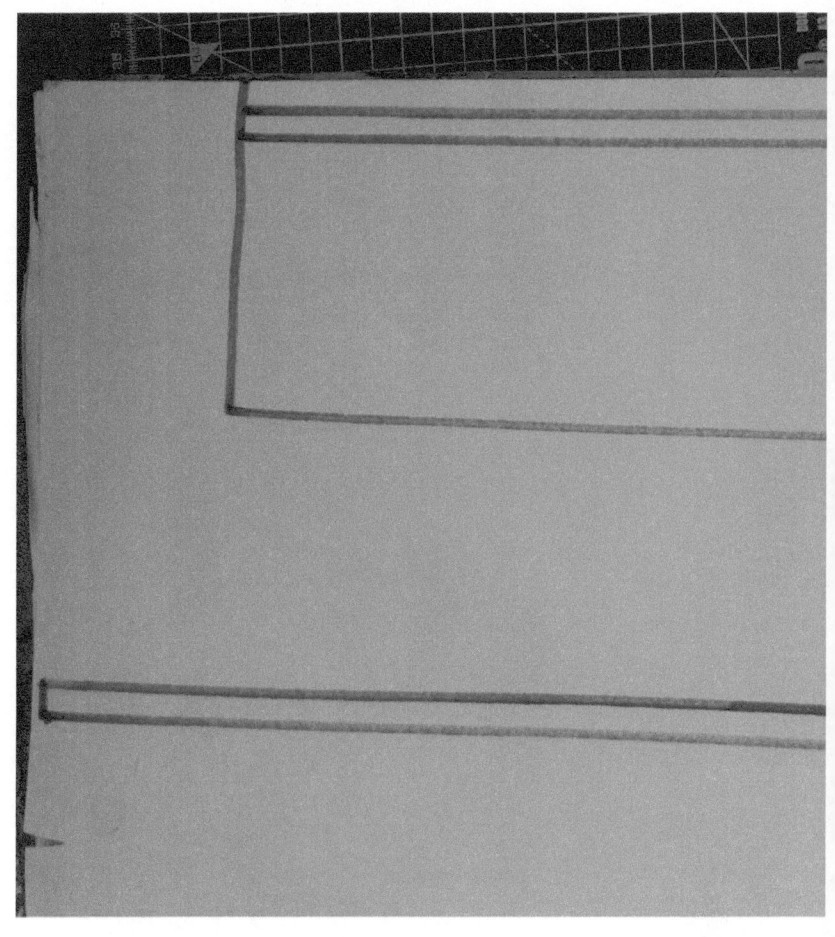

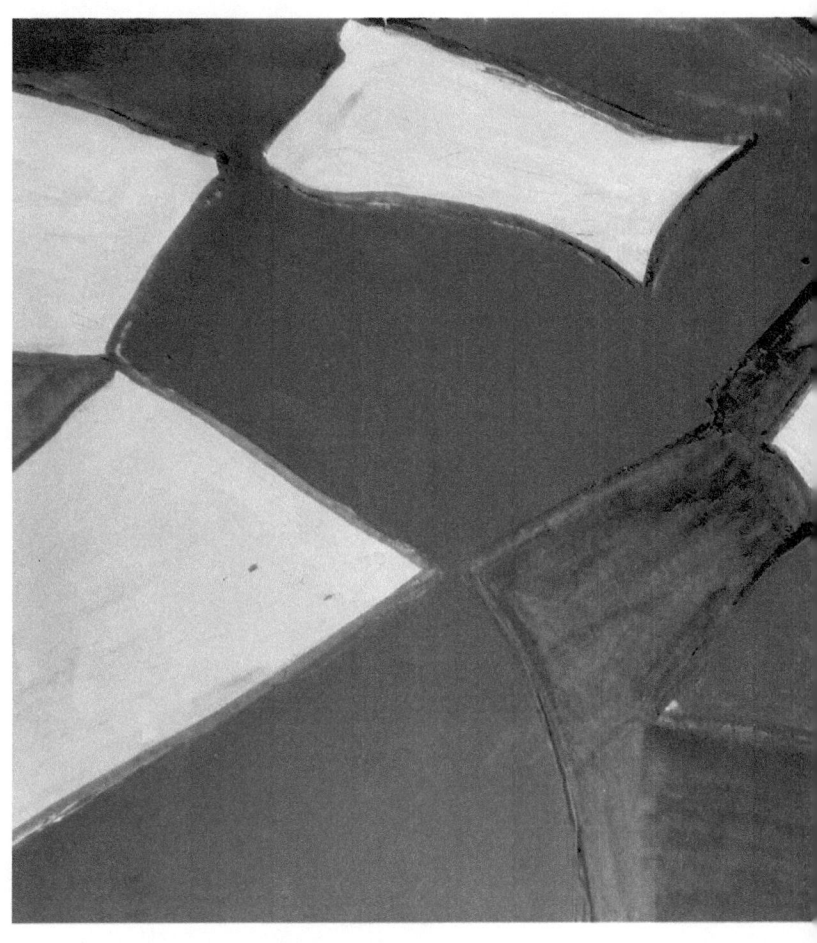

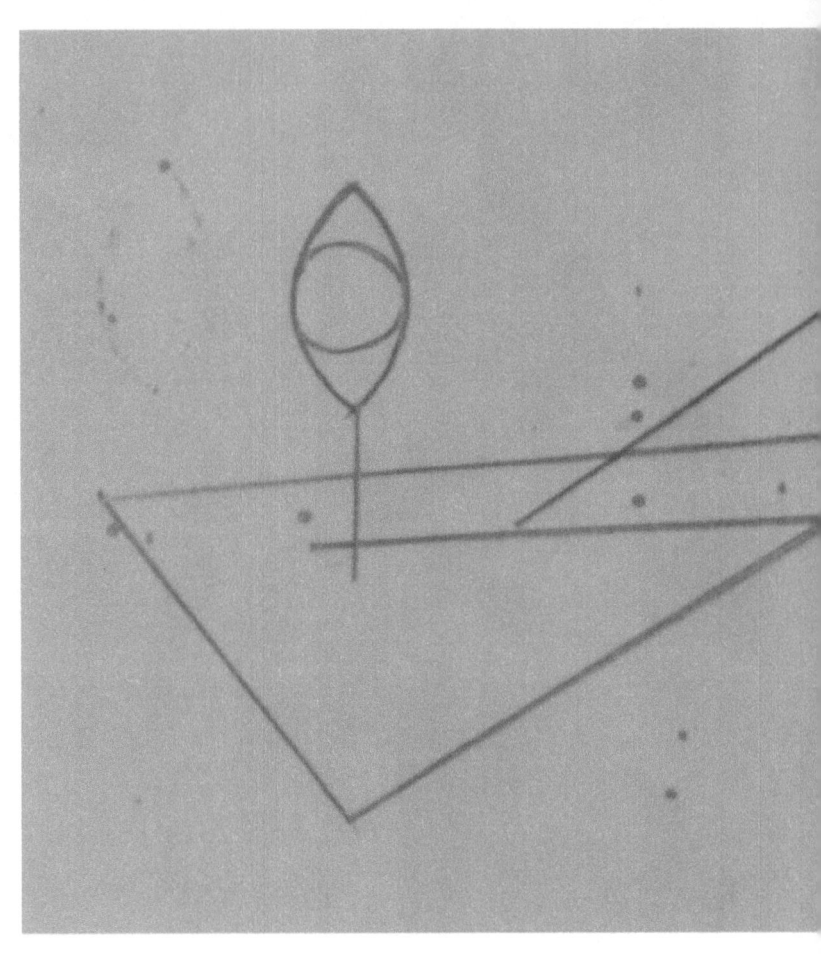

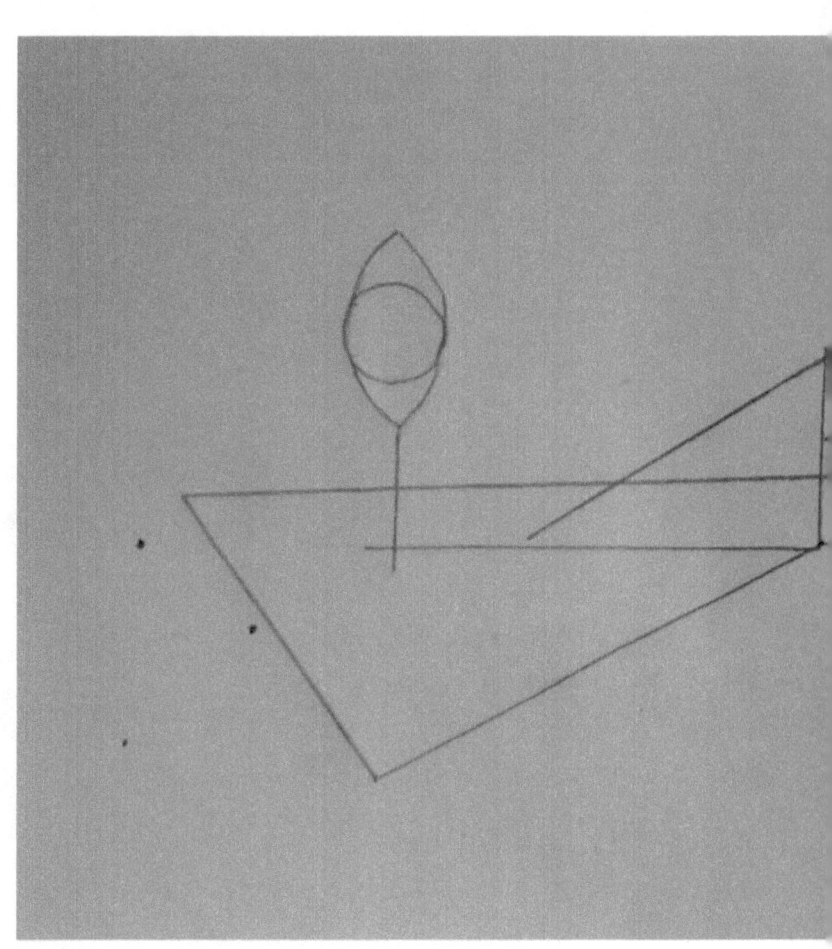

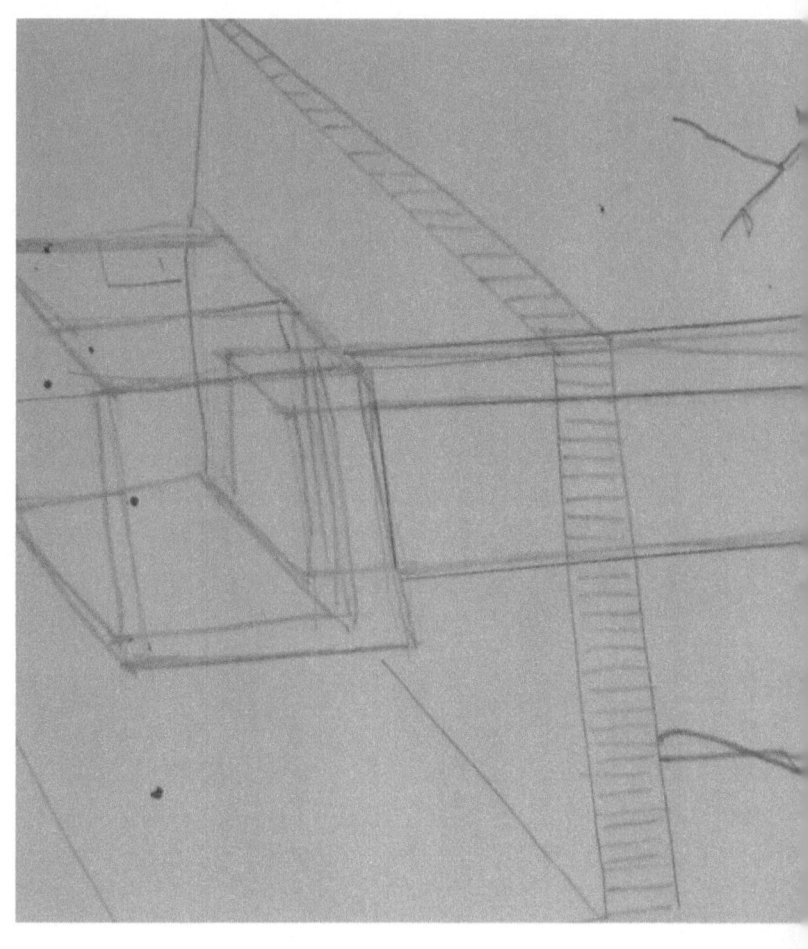

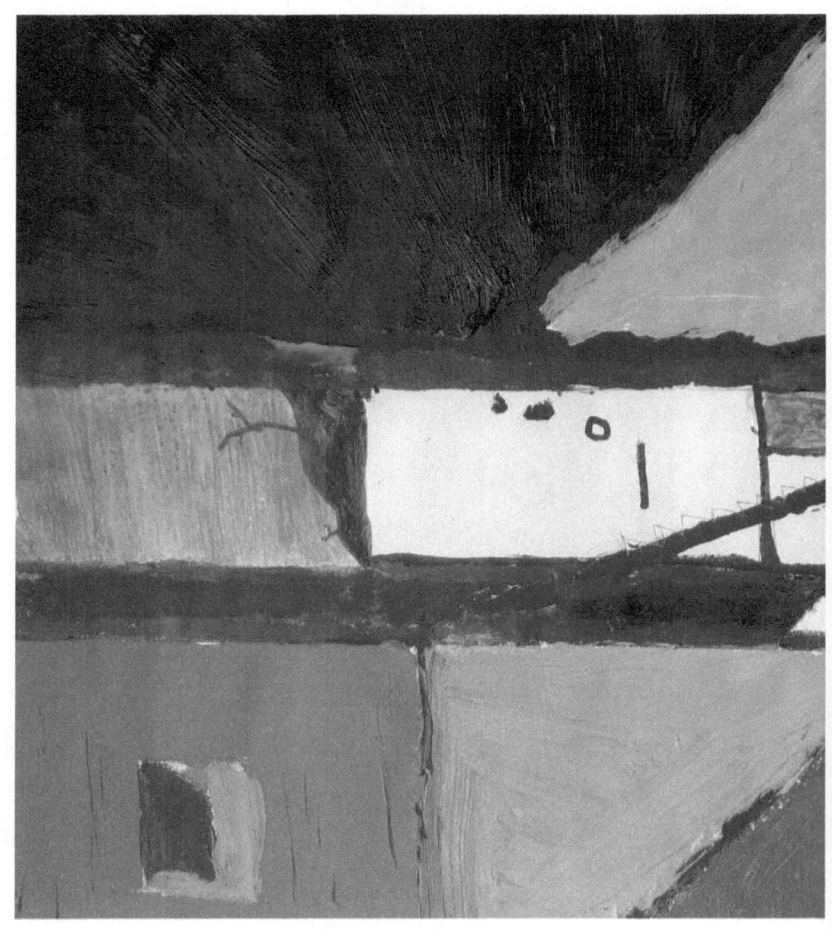

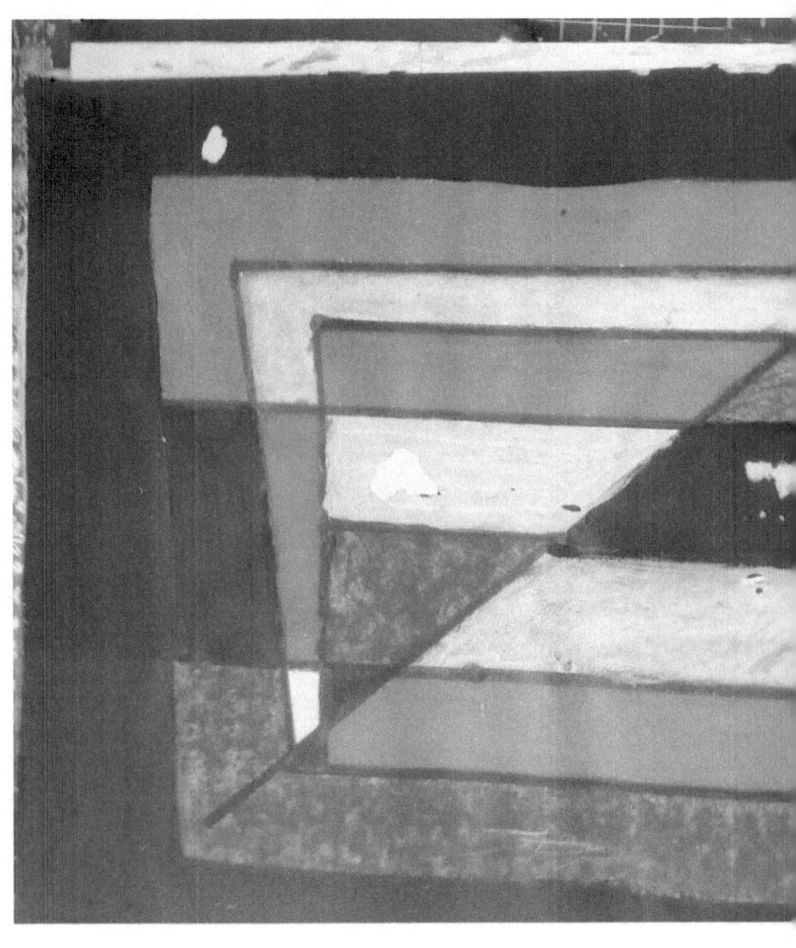

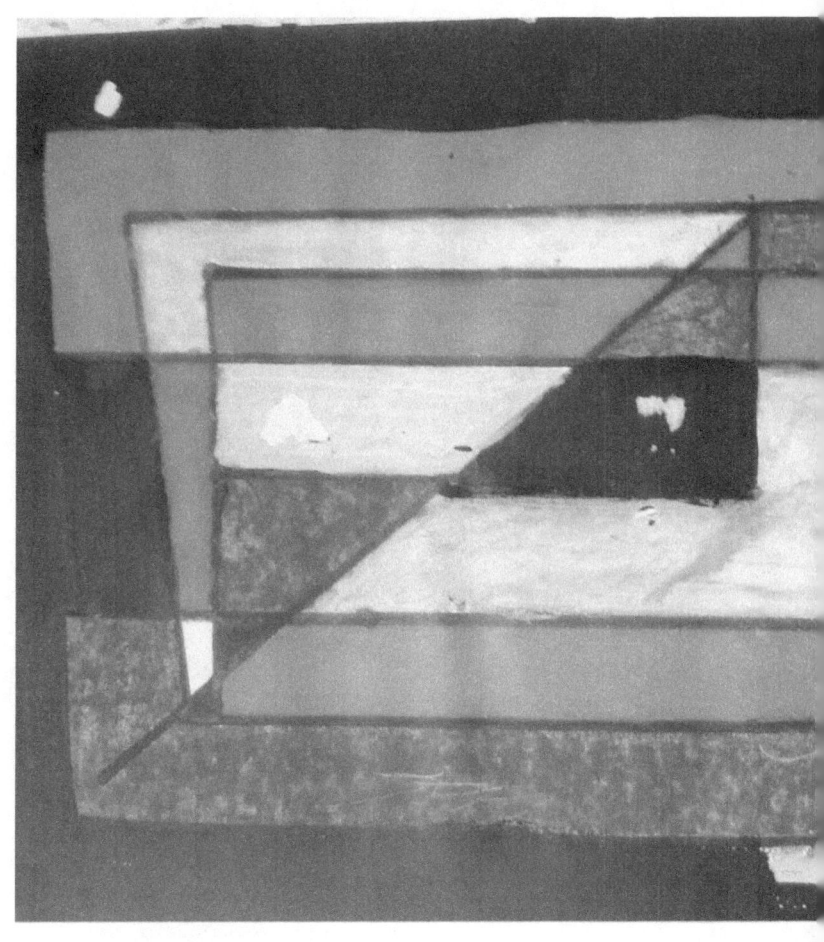

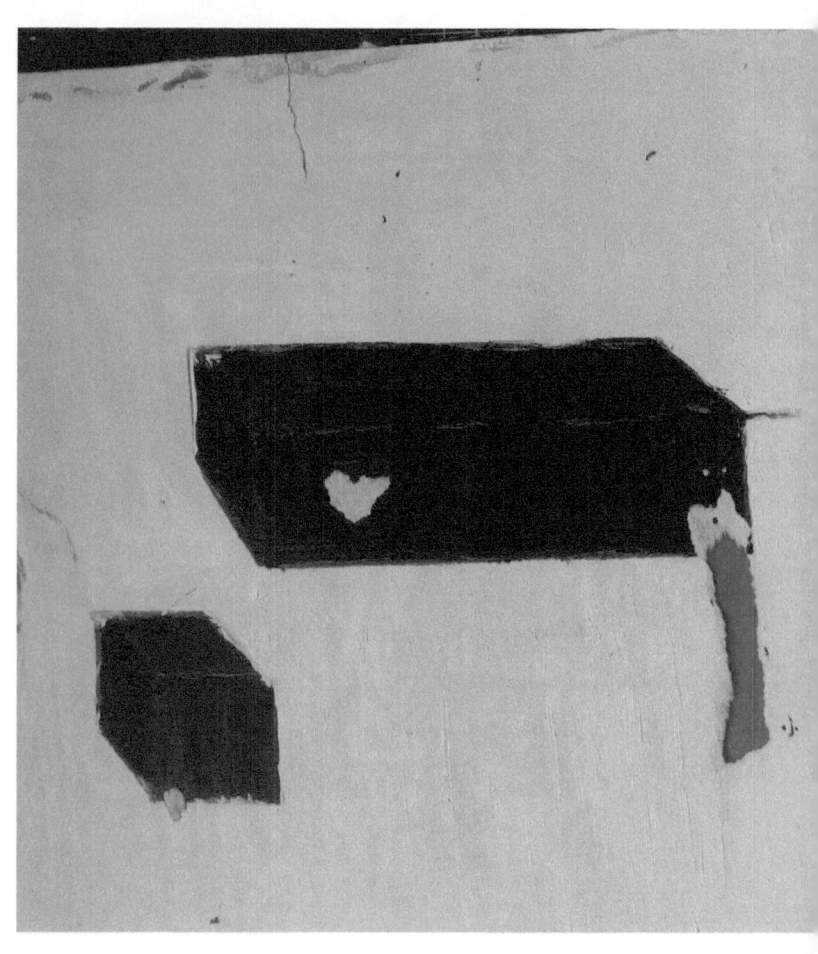

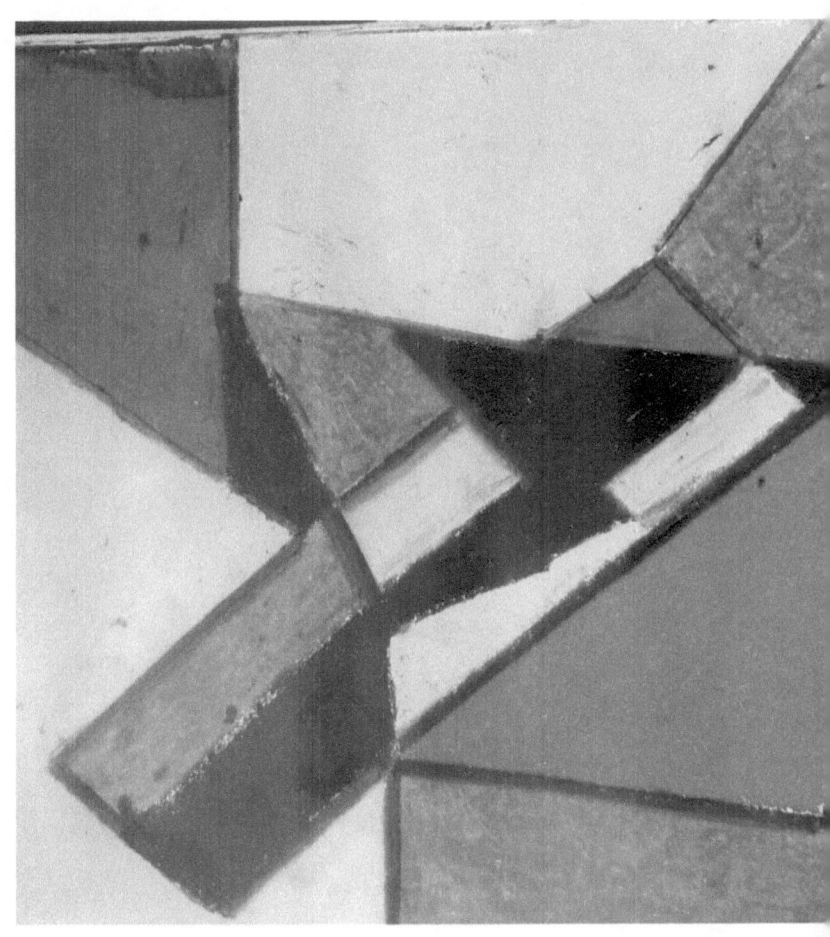

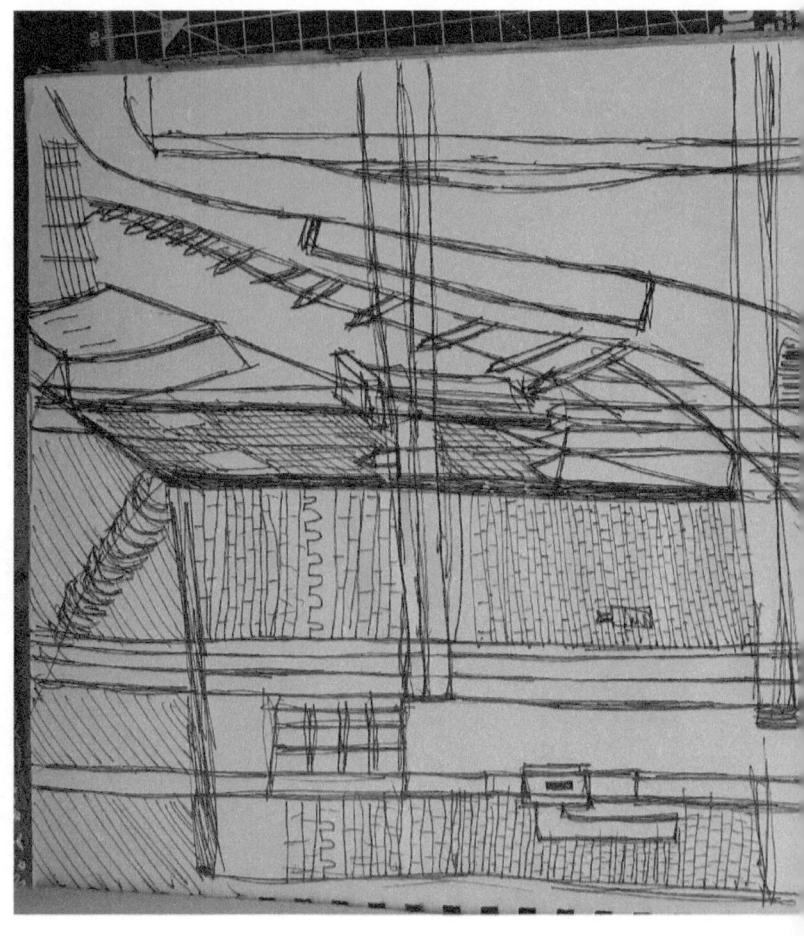

www.ingramcontent.com/pod-product-compliance
Lightning Source LLC
Chambersburg PA
CBHW020434220526
45464CB00002B/695